The Mystery of Christ

The Mystery of Christ

Lance Lambert

LANCE LAMBERT MINISTRIES

Richmond, Virginia, USA

ISBN: 978-1-68389-129-1

www.lancelambert.org

Contents

Introduction

Lance shared a series of messages on the Mystery of Christ at Halford House in Richmond, Surrey, England. These messages have been lightly edited for clarity and included in the contents of this book. We pray you will be encouraged on in your search for the Lord's heart, as we have been in ours through the words shared by Lance in the following pages. May you be blessed and meet the Lord afresh.

the Lance Lambert Ministries team

1.
Mystery

Ephesians 3:1–21

For this cause I Paul, the prisoner of Christ Jesus in behalf of you Gentiles,— if so be that ye have heard of the dispensation of that grace of God which was given me to you-ward; how that by revelation was made known unto me the mystery, as I wrote before in few words, whereby, when ye read, ye can perceive my understanding in the mystery of Christ; which in other generations was not made known unto the sons of men, as it hath now been revealed unto his holy apostles and prophets in the Spirit; to wit, that the Gentiles are fellow-heirs, and fellow-members of the body, and fellow-partakers of the promise in Christ Jesus through the gospel, whereof I was made a minister, according to the gift of that grace of God which was given me according to the working of his power. Unto me, who am less than the least of all saints, was this grace given, to preach unto the Gentiles the unsearchable riches of Christ; and to make all men see what is the dispensation of the mystery which for ages hath been hid in God who created all things; to the intent that now unto the principalities and the powers in the heavenly places might be made known through the church the manifold wisdom of God, according to the eternal purpose which he purposed in Christ Jesus our Lord: in whom we have boldness and access in confidence through our faith in him. Wherefore I ask that ye may not faint at my tribulations for you, which are your glory.

For this cause I bow my knees unto the Father, from whom every family in heaven and on earth is named, that he would grant you, according to the riches of his glory, that ye may be strengthened with power through his Spirit in the inward man; that Christ may dwell in your hearts through faith; to the end that ye, being rooted and grounded in love, may be strong to apprehend with all the saints what is the breadth and length and height and depth, and to know the love of Christ which passeth knowledge, that ye may be filled unto all the fulness of God.

Now unto him that is able to do exceeding abundantly above all that we ask or think, according to the power that worketh in us, unto him be the glory in the church and in Christ Jesus unto all generations for ever and ever. Amen.

Colossians 1:24–2:7
Now I rejoice in my sufferings

for your sake, and fill up on my part that which is lacking of the afflictions of Christ in my flesh for his body's sake, which is the church; whereof I was made a minister, according to the dispensation of God which was given me to you-ward, to fulfil the word of God, even the mystery which hath been hid for ages and generations: but now hath it been manifested to his saints, to whom God was pleased to make known what is the riches of the glory of this mystery among the Gentiles, which is Christ in you, the hope of glory: whom we proclaim, admonishing every man and teaching every man in all wisdom, that we may present every man perfect in Christ; whereunto I labor also, striving according to his working, which worketh in me mightily.

For I would have you know how greatly I strive for you, and for them at Laodicea, and for as many as have not seen my face in the flesh; that their hearts may be comforted, they being knit together in love, and unto all riches of the full assurance of understanding, that they may know the mystery of God, even Christ, in whom are all the treasures of wisdom and knowledge hidden. This I say, that no one may delude you with persuasiveness of speech. For though I am absent in the flesh, yet am I with you in the spirit, joying and beholding your order, and the stedfastness of your faith in Christ.

As therefore ye received Christ Jesus the Lord, so walk in him, rooted and builded up in him, and established in your faith, even as ye were taught, abounding in thanksgiving.

Shall we just bow together in prayer and really ask the Lord to grant to us that spirit of wisdom and revelation?

Lord, we just bow here in Thy presence, and we want to confess and recognise before Thee, Lord, that unless Thou art here, and unless the Holy Spirit really does fulfil His ministry amongst us in leading us into the truth as it is in Jesus, then Lord, we know that this time will be without real and eternal value. But Lord, if Thou art here, then it means Thy Word will live to us. It will come to dwell in us richly in all wisdom and knowledge. Lord, there will be a consequence and a result of the speaking of Thy Word. To that end, Lord, we appeal to Thee: make Thy presence the reality of this time, we ask. As we come to Thy Word, Lord, we take that anointing which we need for speaking and for hearing. Lord, wilt Thou do something in our hearts? For those who may feel they know something about this matter, bring it with such freshness and vitality, oh Lord, that it will come with a greater discovery of Thyself. For those who do not understand it at all, we pray it may not be overwhelming, but rather Lord, it may come as a ray of light into the heart. In Thy light, then we shall see light. Oh Lord, it will be a progressive light, growing as it were unto full noon day. Dear Lord, do this we pray. Make this a time of revelation and illumination. Thou canst draw so near to us, that Lord, something happens in our hearts that will make it all worthwhile. We shall give Thee all the praise, and all the glory, in the name of Thy Son, our Lord Jesus, Amen.

I would like to talk about a matter which is generally relegated to what is called the deepest of the deeper teaching. People tend to feel, "Oh, dear! To begin talking on a matter like that, we will be lost right from the start." But I don't believe so at all. I believe that the Lord can give us such help, such grace, such illumination and revelation, that we shall begin to see something clearly as we have never seen it before.

The days in which we are living require clarity of vision. We live in the midst of people, believing people, who are used to contradicting what they believe in practice. There is a spirit that has gone right through Christianity that we believe wonderful things, we believe in ideals, we believe in tremendous truths. However, as for the practice of it and the experience of it, it would shock us if in actual fact it were to be so. Of course, it is very easy for us to blame everybody else and to say, "Well, of course they don't practice what they preach." The fact comes down to you. Anyone who says of somebody else, "they don't practice what they preach" is normally not practicing what *they* preach. In other words, in the final analysis, the only way you and I ever really become aware of truth is not just by the preaching of words, or the preaching of truths. It is because the truth has got into that person like fire and somehow then the words and the preaching coalesce and somehow, we are affected. When we see a life, however weak and with whatever number of failings, in which the Lord is dwelling, and in which the Lord is manifesting Himself, we all recognise this.

Now, this is what we really need. So I am going to embark upon a matter which I shall explore a little by the grace of God. We shall start on the foundation of the whole thing. Later, we shall come right down to the practical relevance of all this in our life as the people of God—in your life, in my life, in our family life, and in every aspect of our life.

The Foundation

Now, the phrase that has been so much with me is this little phrase in Ephesians 3:4:

whereby, when you read, ye can perceive my
understanding in the mystery of Christ.

This chapter three of the Ephesian letter is a parenthesis. In other words, the apostle Paul was writing or dictating this letter and when he got to what we call chapter three, verse one, "For this cause I, Paul, the prisoner of Christ Jesus, on behalf of you Gentiles," he suddenly broke off on a digression! Then in chapter four, verse one, he comes back again, "I, therefore the prisoner in the Lord, beseech you to walk worthily of the call, wherewith you were called." This chapter three is a kind of heavenly digression.

Now, many preachers are guilty of digressions—not always heavenly—but most preachers are, at one time or another, drawn off on this way or drawn out on that way and digress from the matter. Having said that in one sense it is a heavenly digression, a kind of parenthesis that is in brackets, do not for one single moment think that it is just a confused jumble of thoughts out of the apostle's mind—not at all. This digression actually comes to the very heart of the matter.

As is so often with the apostle's asides, it comes right behind the scenes to the whole matter that lies behind this Ephesian letter, and indeed, behind everything. So it is not to be overlooked or to be treated as of secondary importance, as though his real theme, which he began in chapter one and two and which he goes on with in chapter four and five, is the main, fundamental matter and that this digression is secondary—no, not at all. It is as if the apostle draws aside the veil of the Holy of Holies and takes us from the Holy Place into the most holy place of all. It is as if, suddenly, by the Spirit in this digression, in a flash of divine inspiration, he brings us immediately to the heart of the whole matter. That, I find, is tremendous.

The Significance of Salvation

What is the significance of your salvation, the real significance? I don't mean salvation in that you have been saved. Some people think that is the significance—"I've been saved! I've been saved from sin. I've been saved from hell!" But what is the real, eternal significance of your salvation as far as God is concerned? Why did God bother about us useless little bits of clay? Why did He labour with us, when He could, with one single word, have cancelled out everything and started all over again? What is the significance of your salvation? What is the real significance of Christ's coming into this world and of His finished work on the cross?

The Significance of God's Dealings

What is the real significance of all God's dealings with mankind? Why did he start with Adam and when Adam and Eve failed, why did he go on with Abel? Then later with Shem? Then with Abraham? Then after Abraham, with Isaac, with Jacob, with Joseph, and on through all the great line of the people of God? What was it that He was doing? What is the key to it all?

The Significance of History

What is the significance of history itself? Is the history of the nations just one sort-of coincidental mass of details? Or is the history of the nations something over which God rules with something (like the apple of His eye) in His mind the whole time? In other words, it is not just that God has an eternal object in eternity, outside of time, but time *itself* is related to that objective of God. What is the significance then, of history itself, of the nations, of the world, of all the great empires that have come and gone? of Israel—its exile, its regathering, and its final salvation and destiny? What is the significance of the creation of this universe and of mankind? Why did God begin the whole matter? Why has He persevered?

Now I believe that the little phrase "the mystery of Christ" introduces us to the heart of this matter. We come to the answer to all these questions in this little phrase "the mystery of Christ." For instance, in Ephesians 3:3–5, "how that by revelation was made known unto me the mystery, as I wrote before in few words, whereby, when ye read, ye can perceive my understanding in the mystery of Christ; which in other generations was not made known unto the sons of men, [from Adam until that time] as it hath now been revealed unto his holy apostles and prophets in the Spirit." Then he explains it: "to wit, that the Gentiles, are fellow-heirs, and fellow-members of the body, and fellow-partakers of the promise in Christ Jesus."

Now, I don't know what that means to you, but evidently this whole mystery of the Messiah has to do with the Gentiles becoming fellow-heirs, fellow-members of the body. That was an altogether new phrase never before used: "fellow-members of the body and fellow-partakers of the promises." What promises? All the promises God made to the patriarchs, to the fathers; all the promises God made to the prophets, to Israel, to His chosen people, to His elect people. Well, I say, that is something worth considering. This thing that has been hidden for generations has now been revealed. But is it not a tragedy that the vast majority of Christian believers have no idea as to the mystery of Christ? In fact, most of them will say, "Oh dear, that is too theological for me." They would creep away. And yet, if I understand what the apostle Paul is saying, he is telling us that this is the birthright of every child of God.

Then look again in the same chapter, Ephesians 3:9–11. Listen to these marvellous words. This is the apostle again speaking, he says: "and to make all men see what is the dispensation of the mystery which for ages hath been hid in God."

What a wonderful phrase! Have you ever thought about it? Which for ages has been hid? Where has it been hid? Hid in God. So it has come out of His heart. It has come out of not only His mind, but out of His heart. It has been hid in Him, locked up within the very being of God. So this is no small matter. This is something absolutely tremendous. This is something essential, something fundamental. It has been locked up in the very being of God and now, the apostle says, "It is my job to make all men see what is the dispensation."

The word *dispensation* is a dreadful word—one of those theological words. I think it is unfortunate that the word used is *dispensation* because people get the idea of dispensational truth, and they carve everything up into so many ages. Now, there may be truth in that, but I think it is a shame that as soon as we use the word dispensation people get a kind of connotation. I think it is rather good in the New American Standard Bible where it says, "to make all men see what is the administration of this mystery, which has been hidden for ages in God." You see, the word is *management*, it is household management. The word has the idea of the running of the household, the administration of a household, the sort-of watching. *Stewardship* is another word that could be used—the stewardship of the mystery. He says, to make all men see, what is the stewardship of this mystery, what is the administration of this mystery which has been hid for ages in God.

Then he goes on, "... who created all things ..." So, we get a hint there, that God created all things with this mystery locked up in His heart. This mystery, this secret, was the real significance of why He created all things: the universe, the things which are seen, the things which are not seen, mankind itself.

God's Purpose from Eternity Past

Now he goes on:

> ... to the intent that now unto the principalities and the
> powers in the heavenly places might be made known through
> the church the manifold wisdom of God, according to the
> eternal purpose which he purposed in Christ Jesus our Lord.

Here is another wonderful word: He purposed something in Christ Jesus our Lord. It was not some coincidental purpose.

It was not some secondary purpose. It was not some subsidiary purpose. It was the eternal purpose of God. That is going right back before times eternal. God had a design, a plan, an objective, an ultimate goal. In the light of this design He created the universe, all things that can be seen, as well as not seen, things visible and things invisible. Then He created mankind. When mankind fell, He already had in His heart, the whole answer to the fall in the person of His own Son. Well, that is very wonderful. It is rather a lot. It is almost overwhelming! But it is rather wonderful that it says, "according to the eternal purpose which He purposed in Christ Jesus our Lord."

Those of you who have the Revised Standard Version will see that it very beautifully puts it like this: "according to the eternal purpose which He realised in Christ Jesus our Lord." So it is not only that He purposed this in Christ Jesus our Lord, but the Lord Jesus was, as it were, the foundation, the basis for the whole matter, but more than that, He realised it in Christ Jesus our Lord. Not just through Him, but in Him He has realised something. The very thing that God wanted from the start for mankind, for the universe, He has secured in the Lord Jesus; He has realised in the Lord Jesus. Now, those of you who have got the New American Standard Bible will see that it is rather awkwardly translated, but I think very tellingly translated. It says, "according to the eternal purpose, which He carried out in Christ Jesus our Lord."

Now, I do not know what you feel, but I think that those few scriptures alone, just make me stand back and think, "My word, what is in this matter? There is something tremendous in this matter." It makes no difference whether you are an aged saint, or a person who has just been saved a day ago, or an hour ago, there is something in here for us if we are saved. There is something tremendous in this for us. We are involved with this. This is not something that is just left for theological minds, for those who go to Theological Seminary. This is meant to be the kind of revelation that puts a dynamic into our living, and an impetus into our service. This is the kind of thing which gives us a goal, it gives us a horizon, it lifts us out of one dimension into another. It is something which suddenly gives us as it were, the whole thrust of our worship and of our service.

Let me just put it like this: I cannot help but worship a God who has a heart like that. It would be marvellous enough if God was just sentimental, and had in some corner of His heart some sentiment for me and saved me. But when I think that God has a plan for the whole universe, and for mankind, and in spite of its fall, He has somehow or other laid a foundation through which He can reconcile the whole thing back to Himself, to bring it back to Himself, and then finally fulfil His purpose, that is tremendous!

That lifts this whole matter onto another level, doesn't it? instead of the normal kind of thing we get in Christian circles, where we talk about streets of gold, and pearly gates and angels dancing round with harps and trumpets, and the saints sitting on damp clouds in glorified nighties singing, "Hallelujah" forever and ever. I mean, you can understand the world sort of thinking that we are old fashioned squares who should have gone out with Queen Victoria. This kind of revelation is the kind of light that brings scope into our service, and scope into our Christian life and living. It gives us perhaps a glimmer of an understanding.

Expressions of This Mystery

Marriage

Now, let's come back again to this matter. It is not only in this chapter. If we turn to Ephesians 5:32, we find that here the apostle Paul has been talking about marriage. When he talks about marriage, he comes to this in verse 32: "this mystery is great, but I speak in regard of Christ and of the church." Now in this incredible chapter in talking about husbands loving their wives, and wives being subject to their husbands, and husbands treating their wives as their own flesh, their own body, the apostle Paul says, "You see, this whole matter of marriage is an expression in time of an eternal reality that is in the heart of God." He ends by saying, "this mystery is great, that two can become one flesh." He says, "This mystery is great, but I speak in regard of Christ and of the church." What does he mean? Listen to it, he means that we have not just become fellow-partakers of promises given to the Fathers and to the Prophets, to the people of God under the Old Covenant. We have not only become fellow-heirs with them of all that God has, as it were, made a heritage for His Son. We have become fellow-members of His body. That's the heart of the matter.

The Body—Bone of His Bone

In other words, the Lord Jesus looks upon every born-again child of God as His own flesh. Remember when Saul of Tarsus was on his way to Damascus, somewhere along the Golan Heights, and was struck down by a revelation of the Lord Jesus. When he saw light that shone greater than the midday sun (and the midday sun is something in those parts with no mist nor upper vapor to make it easier), he heard that voice saying "Saul, Saul, why persecutest thou me?"

Saul said, "Who are you, Lord?"

This heavenly One said, "I am Jesus, whom you persecute. It is hard for you to kick against the goad."

You know, it was the beginning of a revelation. Later on, the apostle Paul said in his Galatian letter, "When it pleased God ... to reveal His Son in me ..." You might wonder when that happened. It went back to his very conversion, and perhaps again after when he went into the desert of Arabia for those three years and pondered and pondered and pondered. It must have come to him again and again, "How could I have persecuted Jesus? He wasn't there. It was those disciples that I persecuted. I know it was wrong, but it was the disciples I hounded to death, that I brought a false witness against, that I did this and this and this and this." Then it must have come as a revelation to him: "No, when I touched the most insignificant one of those disciples, the most ignorant one of those disciples, the most unworthy one of those disciples, I touched Jesus. It was as if they were His body. It was as if they were His flesh. When I martyred them, I martyred Him and when I beat them, I beat Him and when I rejected them, I rejected Him and when I tortured them, I tortured Him."

So He said, "Saul, Saul, why persecutest thou Me?"

That is the mystery of Christ, oh glory! It would transform every life in this room if we saw it—but we don't. Few of us really see it. We think we see it. We mentally appreciate it, but few have ever really seen it. It is like a spiritual blockbuster when we suddenly realise what union with God really means. We suddenly realise what union with Christ really means! We have become His body, we have become His members, we have become His limbs, we have become partakers of the divine nature. Somehow, we have been introduced into God's Christ.

We are *in* Him. It is tremendous!

So the apostle speaks of this mystery. He says, "This mystery is great." Just as woman was taken out of Adam, bone and flesh, out of his open side, so the apostle John, in the 19th chapter of his gospel says, "One of the soldiers went up and pierced His side with a spear, and forthwith there came out, blood and water." Then as if it meant a tremendous amount to John the apostle he said, "And I who bear witness, my witness is true." Most people would say, "Well, what is he getting so excited about? The thing to get excited about is that Jesus uttered the cry, 'Finished!' That's the thing to get excited about." But not John. John was not only excited about the word "finished," he said, "You know what it was? His side was open, and out of it came blood and water." Later, writing a letter he said there were three things: "blood and water and spirit."

What he was really saying was: This is the last Adam. This is the second Man. He was put to sleep on the cross. When He said "Finished," He died! His eyes closed, His spirit went, and His side was opened, and out of His side was taken the church, the bride. She came out through blood and water, created out of Him, out of His life, out of His nature, out of His sacrifice, out of His death, so that when He was raised from the dead, it was as if He said, "This is flesh of My flesh and bone of My bone." On the day of Pentecost, when He obtained the promised

Holy Spirit from the Father and poured out the Holy Spirit upon the whole church, it was as if He was saying, "Flesh of my flesh, bone of my bone. This is Me."

"This mystery is great," said the apostle, "but I speak of Christ and the church." Oh, if we believers only saw what a wonderful thing this is, how tremendous this is, how it would revolutionise not only our lives, but our living.

He Purposed ...

Then, of course, I think of Ephesians 1:9–11 in the same connection. This is where the apostle had introduced this matter, but I think when you don't get hold of his marvellous digression in chapter three, this becomes very heavy. But listen to it as he puts it now in the light of what I have said:

> making known unto us the mystery of his will, according
> to his good pleasure which he purposed in him unto a
> dispensation of the fulness of the times, to sum up all things
> in Christ, the things in the heavens, and the things upon the
> earth; in him, I say, in whom also we were made a heritage,
> having been foreordained according to the purpose of him
> who worketh all things after the counsel of his will;

Well, I find that absolutely marvellous. It means that your salvation, your conversion was not some afterthought of God where He sort-of saw you in an evangelistic meeting and said, "Oh, so-and-so looks interested! I'll save them." According to this, it says you were foreordained in some unfathomable way that you and I will never be able to understand. Somewhere back there before times eternal, God knew us all. Now, since this is wonderful, don't you think there is a reason for you and me to start sitting up about it and saying, "Do I understand this?" Maybe mentally you appreciate it, but get rid of that mental business. Mentally appreciated truth is grave clothes. Whenever we "get" something only in our head, it ties us, inhibits us, binds us, darkens us. It is only when it comes by *divine* illumination that suddenly it lives and we see it and then we are alive to God. It becomes power, and life and grace. I do not care who you are, or however long you have been walking with the Lord, ask Him for fresh revelation on this matter. Let the Lord shine into your heart on this matter.

Take those words in Colossians 1:26 and listen to what the apostle says here that again is very interesting. He speaks about difficult things, things that are beyond the ordinary. He speaks about filling up in his flesh, what remains of the sufferings of Christ, for the body's sake, which is the church. I doubt whether anybody has really fully understood what that means, except that in some way, our Lord has left a little residue of suffering, which He calls His own sufferings, and He says, "You can come into the fellowship of it if you want to." What is it all for? Something so deep, something so profound, something so unusual? What is it for? He says:

> ... *the dispensation of God which was given me to you-*
> *ward, to fulfil the Word of God, even the mystery*
> *which hath been hid for ages and generations.*

He said ages and generations. Generations are one thing ... ages are another! So that means all the ages and generations.

> *hid for ages and generations, but now hath*
> *it being manifested to His saints*

It is not just to the special ones, those that the Popes have at one time or another canonised (many of whom have now been found never to have existed in the first place). These of whom he spoke are biblical saints, those who God has saved, God has sanctified. Now what happens? Look again.

> *But now hath it been manifested to his saints, to whom*
> *God was pleased to make known what is the riches of*
> *the glory of this mystery among the Gentiles ...*

I find that very wonderful: this "mystery among the Gentiles." What it really means is that if you are a Christian, you are not a Gentile. You are in the Israel of God. You have been introduced into something else: "this mystery among the Gentiles which is Christ in you." In the Greek "in you" is in the plural. It is: "in you all." Not just in me personally, but in you, and you, and you, and you, and you, and you. Christ in you all, the hope of glory. So there we have something else about this mystery.

This Strategic Purpose

If you go on, of course, then the apostle starts to talk about the personal side. He says, "and we labour day and night," why? "... that we might present every man perfect in Christ," in this Messiah. Then he goes on in the next paragraph, "that they may know the mystery of God, even Christ in whom are all the treasures of wisdom and knowledge hidden." Now, we have to underline the simple fact that the way in which the apostle introduces this matter of the mystery of Christ is not some optional truth, glorious, but not fundamental. He presents it as something which is vital and fundamental to our whole understanding of God's purpose, fundamental to our whole understanding of the age in which we live, in which we are found. In other words, and I use the word carefully, it is in fact, strategic.

This whole matter of the mystery of Christ being revealed to us, being manifested to us, made known to us is to do with the strategy of God. It is not just the strategy of God for a few people in a particular generation, but a strategy of God in saving mankind through His Son, in redeeming the church, which is His body.

Now, I do not know how much that means to you, but have you ever really understood what this word *mystery* means? What does it mean? In common usage, the word mystery means: "a secret for which no answer can be found, for which no explanation is adequate."

Shall I say that again? In common usage, when we use the word mystery, we mean a secret for which no answer can be found and for which, no explanation is adequate. For example, say some people are speaking about some sort of happenings in some so-called "haunted house," and the scientists all go down there, and then they say, "It is a mystery." They have ideas, but their ideas do not constitute an answer and their explanation is not adequate to the facts. Now, it is not just that, there are all sorts of other things which they call mysteries. But whenever they say something is a mystery they mean that, at present, its explanation eludes us.

Initiated

Now, that is the way most believers consider the mystery of Christ, something that eludes them ... and that is the tragedy. They have taken a completely contemporary idea of the word mystery and transferred it. For them, it is something that God has made a secret for which there is no answer, something for which no answer can be found and for which no explanation is adequate. Yet that is not the meaning of this word. In biblical usage, particularly the New Testament, the Greek word means "that which is known only to the initiated." That means something a little different. *That which is known only to the initiated.* This will horrify some people, but it is just as well, because some people get so worked up on pagan things. They say, "Oh, dear, dear, dear! You can't use any pagan sort of thing!" But you see, the New Testament uses lots of words that had pagan origin, and this is one of them. In classical Greek, this word would have meant: *to initiate into the Greek mystery religions.* The apostle Paul knew all about that. It was a very common thing, because there were all kinds of secret religious societies and you had to be "initiated into the mysteries." It is very interesting really, because only the initiated could share an understanding of whatever it was. Do you see? Now, the apostle Paul makes actual references and uses the very word in Philippians 4:12:

I know how to be abased, and I know also how to abound:
in everything and in all things have I learned the secret.

That in the Greek is this: *I have been initiated.* I have been
initiated. This is the root of this word, translated, *mystery*.
It is to be initiated. So, much more than getting the idea that it
is something withheld from you, it is something into which you
are initiated. Perhaps you do not like that word initiated. Shall
we say *introduced*? Into which you have been brought? Into which
you have been introduced? When we begin to see it like that,
it transforms the whole thing. The Holy Spirit uses this word with
the emphasis, as *Vines* says, not on knowledge withheld, but on
truth revealed.

Then comes the punch. We thus discover that nearly all the
special terms associated with this word in the New Testament,
are all to do with our understanding. Notice this: we were taught
that the mystery is *made known* unto us or *manifested* to us or
revealed to us or *preached* to us, or we are told that whereby you
can perceive by *understanding* of the mystery. The emphasis is not
on that it is withheld, but that it is communicated. Now, I find
this really rather wonderful that every born-again believer is an
initiate in this matter. You haven't got to be special, you haven't
got to be elite. You haven't got to be one of the overcomers. If you
are born of God you are a candidate for being introduced into
this truth that God has revealed and wants to illuminate for you.
Therefore, we have to ask.

You see so many of us have this strange idea ... people always
come to me and say, "You know, God has never spoken to me
in my life." Well, of course not! I knew a boy once who actually

became deaf because he did not want to hear. He grew up in a noisy family and he did not particularly like his father or his mother. So he developed a kind of a mental deafness, which finally became a physical deafness. Do you know there are thousands of believers like that? It is not that they do not want to believe, but they have a funny idea that God will never ever speak to them. "Oh, He'll speak to Lance, and He'll speak to Ron and He would probably speak to some of the others. But to me? I mean, God will never speak to me."

We have the same idea about this matter of the mystery. We say, "He would not reveal it to me. He might if I was a Watchman Nee, or Amy Carmichael, or one of the great men and women in the church militant; He might then consider revealing it to me. But not to me." But just wait. If you are born again, you are a candidate. The only ground that God requires is that you have been saved by His grace, and if you have been saved by His grace, you are a saint. That is your standing. You may not be a saint yet in character, but your standing is that and if your standing is that, your birthright is this: God wants to make known to you this mystery among the Gentiles.

Well, again I say, to me this is something very, very wonderful. You see, even in the Old Testament, you have got the same thing. The Hebrew equivalent of this Greek word is an Aramaic word *raz*. It has been translated in our Bible in Daniel 2:28 in pretty much the same way:

but there is a God in heaven that revealeth secrets,

That is the same word, only in Hebrew.

and he hath made known to the king Nebuchadnezzar
what shall be in the latter days.

Then in verse 47, listen to what the king says:

The king answered unto Daniel, and said, Of a truth your
God is the God of gods, and the Lord of kings, and a revealer
of secrets, seeing thou hast been able to reveal this secret.

The Holy Spirit uses the term of "truth" which cannot be naturally understood, but has to come through revelation. No one can naturally understand God's salvation. It has to come through revelation. The mystery of the gospel has to be revealed to every one of us. We can go from Sunday school and know it all but there comes a moment when suddenly the light shines, and now we say, "Ah! I see it!" Then what we have heard for years is translated into living—the mystery of the gospel, God initiates us, He introduces us, He brings us in. But then there are many other things that we have to take note of, really, the thought behind it. I asked a brother if he would like to think for a few moments and look up some of the things on this matter, and he did. This is what he said, which I think is very helpful. He said, "Well, the best way to put it is this: it is a secret revealed as a privilege to the initiated." Well, I think that is very wonderful.

Then, note its use in the New Testament. I will just give you the scriptures. Here you have got all the kinds. For instance, in Matthew 13:11 we read of the mysteries of the kingdom. "Unto you hath it been given to know the mysteries of the kingdom of heaven." But to the rest—parables. Unto you hath been given to know the mysteries of the kingdom. Not mystery (singular), but the *mysteries* of the kingdom—the secrets of the kingdom! Then what about 1 Corinthians 4:1, when the apostle Paul speaks of them being ministers of Christ and stewards of the mysteries? Oh, I wish there were more servants of the Lord that were stewards of the mysteries. Don't you think so? I mean, if a man has not seen the mysteries himself, how can he communicate them?

Once God has started to show *you* and illuminate you and you begin to see something, you can communicate it to others—although not at once. I always say that when God first reveals something to you, I find it takes two years before you can start talking. To begin with, you only have seen something and you know when other people talk on that subject: "Now, that's not right, that's not right. I know it's not right. I can't put it into words, but it's not right." You can't explain it. If you do, you get tongue tied, and people can tie you up in knots. But after a year or so, suddenly, it is as an open door. You can utter the mystery of Christ, you can begin to communicate it.

Or think of this in Ephesians 3:4. We read of the supreme mystery, the mystery of Christ. In Colossians 2:2, he puts it this way, that they may understand the mystery of God, even Christ. Then comes the most wonderful thing of all, when you have understood that, in Revelation 10. In the midst of all those visions of persecution, martyrdom, dreadful beasts, and dragon serpents, and the whole thing in foment, then we read this wonderful verse in Revelation 10:7, "but in the days of the voice of the seventh angel, when he is about to sound, then is finished the mystery of God, according to the good tidings, which he declared to his servants the prophets."

So the mystery of Christ, the mystery of God, even Christ—it has got to be completed! It is going to be completed in the midst of the whole world in foment. It is going to be completed, according to the good tidings, which He declared to His servants the prophets. It is not going to be less, it is not going to be kind of half done. This work is going to be completed, accomplished, and absolutely perfected. Well, I want to be in that! How can you and I be really in it if we don't even see it? If we have never got on our knees and said to God, "Oh, Lord, You have saved me, but I do not understand this mystery. I want to understand it."

More Mysteries

Israel

Or then think of these other mysteries, I will just give them quickly to you. First: the mystery of Israel—Romans 11. Some people get so tied up on this, it really is a mystery. For them, it is a secret withheld. But it does not have to be. About this, the apostle Paul says, "This mystery is great." Then he talks about "a hardening in part which had befallen Israel, until the fullness of the Gentiles be come in; and so shall all Israel be saved." Some people get tied up in knots over this. When some people heard me before, they asked, "Does it mean then that Israel has got priority over the house of God? Isn't this a little sideline that we are now getting caught up in, distracted into?" What rubbish! It is not Israel and the church. In some wonderful way, in the end, it is Israel and the church come together. That is yet to be. Praise the Lord!

The mystery of Israel is a mystery. It lies behind everything and actually underlies the church. It is the root that carries the church. The church really, in this age are the branches, which are carried by that root. Praise the Lord!

Rapture

Then there is the mystery of the rapture. Well, I am waiting for that. I do not know whether I will get there. Maybe you will be burying me before we come to that rapture, but it doesn't bother me too much, because I think that even if it is a little while, the dead in Christ will rise first. I remember saying that to a dear sister when she knew she was going. "We won't get there before you." She lived her whole life in the light of the coming of the Lord. But you know, when the Lord comes the dead in Christ will rise first, and then we which are alive and remain shall be caught up. We will not prevent them. They will be there first!

Then the apostles says, "Behold, I tell you a mystery. We shall not all sleep, but in the twinkling of an eye, we shall all be changed." The dead in Christ and those who are alive at His coming, their bodies will go through a transfiguration in a moment of time—suddenly the body of sin is changed! People say such silly things. For instance at a funeral—I don't like the word funeral—but you know what I mean. They say, "What does it matter?" Listen, don't you understand, that when you come to the end, right at the end, when the Lord comes, if you are alive it is your actual body that is transfigured? Is there another body that comes down and the Lord says, "Kick that one out of the way!" and down comes the other one and you jump into it and sigh, "Ahhhhhh ..." No, this body ... my own! That is the miracle of it! It was your spirit that was dead in sin that was raised and justified, and it was your soul that has been saved, and now it is your actual body—with its sin!

Somehow God drives the sin out and redeems it. In the twinkling of an eye. That is less than half a second. That is a mystery.

I find that it is just as much a mystery to think of the dear apostle Paul and some of the others who have been dust for almost 2000 years (I mean their bodies). Then suddenly when the trumpet sounds and the Word of the Lord ... the dust comes together and the atoms make up the body again and we have a raised body—a resurrection body. I can't wait for it. I think it is so wonderful! Oh, just think of it! You'll just waltz straight through the wall and out the other side, just like our Lord did. He would suddenly come through a wall and stand in the midst, and yet eat a meal. People say, "Oh, are we going to eat?" Yes! Because our Lord ate broiled fish. So I take it that we are going have something to eat. I don't know who's going to do the cooking, but I know that it is not going to be some sort of ether-type existence, floating around as disembodied spirits. I mean, you know that kind of idea that Christians have got, but it's a Greek idea, the kind of idea that we no longer have bodies. God never made us like that. If He wanted to make us angels, He would have made us that way! They are spirits without bodies. God made us spirit, soul, and body.

When Moses went up before Pharaoh he said, "not a hoof nor a horn should be left in Egypt" and dear old Spurgeon, in that great sermon said, "You know what that means? Not a toenail of the believer's body will be left to Satan. Not a hair." And that's what our Lord said! "Not a hair of your head shall perish," He said (Luke 21:18). What it means is this: not a single atom of your body will be left to Satan or to corruption. Not an atom! So amazing was this, that the apostle Paul said, "according to that power, whereby He shall change this vile body into his own likeness." Our salvation is absolutely marvellous.

Well, it is a mystery! That is all I can say. We have been initiated into it. We do not understand exactly how it is going to happen, but at least it has been revealed to us. At least to me it has. I only know I have got a body and I know that this body is not going to be left to Satan. Praise God for that! I am redeemed! Not just what is inside. I am a redeemed being—spirit, soul, and body! Thank God! I've got no part with that evil creation, or with that usurper of the authority of God. I have been redeemed by the blood of the Lamb, by the Passover blood of the Lamb, and I belong to Him. Not a hoof or a horn of me is going to be left in Egypt.

Well, I hope you see that. Make sure you put it in your will that you are getting a decent, proper burial, not just shoved into the ground sort of willy-nilly, thinking: "It doesn't matter. It'll get there." The thing is that we have an amazing connection between this actual body and our resurrection body. Those of us who are alive and remain—it will actually happen! That is why he calls this a mystery. He says, in the twinkling of an eye, we shall all be changed (see 1 Corinthians 15:51–52). It will be amazing, won't it? You with your aches and pains—and me with mine. Suddenly in the twinkling of an eye I shall look at you and say, "Oooohh!" and you will look at me and say, "Wow! What has happened?!" Yet, I suppose we won't have time to be able to do anything like that. We will be with the Lord!

Even More Mysteries

Then, there is the mystery of the faith in 1 Timothy 3:9. That is a very interesting one, the mystery of the faith. Then there is the mystery of godliness in 1 Timothy 3:16. Then there is the mystery of lawlessness—which we shall soon see with our own eyes—the mystery of lawlessness.

My word, I think we need to be initiated. I think a lot of Christians will be taken in by this antichrist if they don't keep alert. If there is enough darkness in them, and enough ignorance, many could be swept along, just like German Christians were swept along by Adolf Hitler. Unless we have been initiated into the mystery, so that we are alive and alert, we have some understanding and an anointing which teaches us what is true and what is a lie, we could be swept along. Now, do you see? This is a great subject, isn't it? It does not seem to me that it is some small matter. It really does seem tremendous.

To Whom are the Mysteries Revealed?

Who are those to whom these mysteries are revealed? Who are the initiated? To whom does God reveal the mystery of Christ? Now, there may be of course many mysteries of the kingdom, but the comprehensive mystery is the mystery of Christ and the answer is very simple. It is twofold. First, we see it is to those who are born of God. It is as simple as that. It is the birthright of every born-again believer. Listen to the words of our Lord in Matthew 13:11:

> *unto you hath it been given to know*
> *the mysteries of the kingdom.*

Now he wasn't just speaking of the twelve apostles, He was speaking of those whom the Father had given Him and whom He was keeping. In that great high priestly prayer in John 17, He said, "I pray not only for them, but for all of those who believe on me through their word" (see verse 20). That is you and me.

Or again, Colossians 1:26–27 it says:

> ... but now hath it been manifested to His saints, to whom
> God was pleased to make known ... what is this mystery.

Has God been pleased to make known what is this mystery to you? Maybe you have never thought about it, never sought Him, never humbled yourself before Him. What a tremendous need then there is to seek the Lord for such illumination and understanding. We do not have a lot of time left to us, but surely one of our great priorities should be to seek the Lord for this, "Lord, give me understanding."

How does it affect our life here? How does it affect our building up? How does it affect our contribution, our participation? What does it mean as far as our gathering together is concerned? What does it mean for my personal life, my business life, my career life? What does it mean for my family life, my home life, my relationships? Surely something that is so comprehensive brings it all within its scope. You are born of God.

The second thing is such revelation and illumination can only come through the person and work of the Holy Spirit. That is why in 1 Corinthians 2:9–12, (it is often misquoted) it speaks of things which God has prepared. Eye has not seen, ear has not heard, heart has not perceived, understood what God has prepared—

but it has been revealed unto us by the Spirit. So it is something that has been revealed; we have received a glimmer of it. Then he says, "We cannot know the things of God except by the Spirit of God, which has been given to us" (see 1 Corinthians 2:11–12). I think that is very, very important, indeed. That is why the apostle Paul prayed that the spirit of wisdom and revelation be granted to them that they might know and then explain all that they should know.

Four Things Needed

I think then we have to recognise just these four things, if we are going to really understand the mystery of Christ. Now, what are these four things? You might say, "Well, isn't that enough? If it's the Holy Spirit who does it and you have to be born again, that's enough." No, that is just the tragedy. I know thousands and thousands of born-again believers who haven't got the slightest idea as to what the mystery of Christ is. It is their birthright. God wants to reveal it to them, yet they don't know. They've never bothered their little heads about it.

There are four things. The first is humility. I don't care who you are. You might have walked with the Lord for years—or seemingly—but where there is no humility, there is no revelation. Our Lord put it so very, very simply in Matthew chapter 11. We normally only think of it as in a gospel context, but it wasn't in the gospel context that He spoke it. Matthew 11:25, Jesus said:

I thank thee, O Father, Lord of heaven and earth,
that thou didst hide these things from the wise and

understanding, and didst reveal them unto babes.

Now a babe is a very defenceless being. No arrogance. No sufficiency. A babe is a very dependent being. Then He goes on:

> *yea, Father, for so it was well-pleasing in thy sight. All*
> *things have been delivered unto me of my Father: and no*
> *one knoweth the Son, save the Father; neither doth any*
> *know the Father, save the Son, and he to whomsoever*
> *the Son willeth to reveal Him. (verses 26–27)*

You can serve and shout and sing and do everything else. But if the Son does not will to reveal to you the Father, and the heart of the Father, you will never see. That brings us to a place of humility. You cannot be arrogant here. You cannot push. You have got to search yourself. You must humble yourself.

And listen to these lovely words, we never read all these verses together:

> *Come unto me, all ye that labor and are heavy laden,*
> *and I will give you rest. Take my yoke upon you, and*
> *learn of me; for I am meek and lowly in heart: and ye*
> *shall find rest unto your souls. For my yoke is easy,*
> *and my burden is light. (Matthew 11:28–29)*

Humility. That is the first thing.

The second thing is recognition. That may sound to you very simple, but the second thing is very important. What do I mean by recognition? In all the places I go to, I rarely ever hear brethren really recognising before God, how unwise they are. I am always surprised because it is the very first lesson I ever learned, the day after I was converted. It was taught me by a Swedish sister who said, "If you ever want to get anywhere with God, there is one thing you must always ask, and that is for wisdom." She turned me to the Book that I had never read in my life, and read out a promise in James 1:5. (I had never heard of James.)

But if any of you lacketh wisdom, let him
ask of God, who giveth to all liberally and
upbraideth not; and it shall be given him.

I do not know what happened, but it burnt itself into my heart and from that day onwards, twice a day, every morning and every evening, when I was 12 years of age, and right the way through, oh! for many years, I used to say, "Lord, Lord, I ask you for wisdom. I have none." You see, I don't think revelation ever comes unless we recognise that we have no natural revelation. It all comes from God.

It says: "If any man lack wisdom." No one is going to ask for wisdom if he does not think there is a need, if he thinks, "Well, I know the Lord." But if you know you lack wisdom, "... let him ask of God, who give it to all men liberally and upbraideth not." That is so beautiful. It is not as if the Lord says, "You are so stupid, always asking for wisdom. Why do you always come back asking for wisdom?" He does not upbraid. The very recognition of our lack of wisdom is enough to touch His Father's heart. That is the second thing.

The third thing is the Holy Spirit. I've already quoted the word in 1 Corinthians 2:12 and 14:

But we received, not the spirit of the world, but the
spirit which is from God; that we might know the
things that were freely given to us of God ...

... the natural man receiveth not the things of the Spirit of God:
for they are foolishness unto him; and he cannot know them,
because they are spiritually judged [spiritually discerned].

So, you will never come into any understanding of the mystery apart from the Holy Spirit. You can settle that right now. You can go to Bible college, Theological Seminary, read theological tomes, and I don't know what else. You can come to every Bible study happening, but until you ask for the Holy Spirit, graciously to be poured out upon you, and to break through all the inhibitions in your life, you cannot go on and on in revelation. Sometimes He is there, but quenched. Sometimes He is there, but locked up. That is the third thing.

The last thing is the cross. You can never really come into an understanding of the mysteries of the kingdom, or the mystery of Christ and of God except through the operation of the cross. Now, you might wonder where that is. It is in II Corinthians 4:6–10. Again, it is often not associated with this, but this is in context:

Seeing it is God, that said, Light shall shine out of
darkness, who shined in our hearts, to give the light of the
knowledge of the glory of God in the face of Jesus Christ.

But we have this treasure in earthen vessels, that the exceeding greatness of the power may be of God, and not from ourselves; we are pressed on every side, yet not straitened; perplexed, yet not unto despair; pursued, yet not forsaken; smitten down, yet not destroyed; always bearing about in the body the dying of Jesus, that the life also of Jesus may be manifested in our body.

You know, light is a wonderful thing, but if you want to know real light, you have got to go the way of the cross. If you want to have a life without any perplexity, without any breaking, without any dying, you will have no revelation. To have revelation, you have to go that way, by the Holy Spirit. It is not that way by which everybody else knows you are going that way, looking grim, dark, and heavy saying, "Ohhh, the way is the cross." That is not the way of the cross. The way of the cross is when the Holy Spirit so fills you that people, when they touch you only touch vitality, life, and joy. It is life in them—death in us. There is something terribly wrong when we touch others and we touch death. If you are really walking the way of the cross, everyone else gets life, and when they touch you, they do not touch death at all. They touch only life. They touch revelation, they touch light, they touch love, they touch power. But for you, personally, inwardly, it may be a very different story. That is revelation. When the apostle Paul was caught up into the third heaven and saw things and things were revealed to him, and he heard things which are not even lawful for a man to utter, then a thorn was given to him, in his flesh, a messenger from Satan, to bring him down. It was always so. The greater the revelation, the more the Lord has to take measures to see that we are kept humble, broken, and dependent.

May the Lord help us in this matter. I have only introduced this. I hope that you will start to explore these things, looking through the scriptures, really asking the Lord, "Give me light on this matter. I want to really know this." Just get this one thing. This is not something which is withheld from you. This is something which God wants to communicate to you in such a way that it floods your whole life and being. May God do it for us all. Let us pray.

Dear Lord, we need such revelation and only Thou canst give it to us. Oh Lord, we pray that every one of us may have an understanding of the mystery of Christ. Dear Lord, oh, that it might be born into our hearts in such a way that it will come as joy and peace and life and power. That we may know the Lord in a deeper way, may discover Him in ways we have never discovered Him before. Use this to that end, Lord, give us a horizon. Give us a goal. Give us some understanding, Lord, of what we are in and help us. We ask all of this in the name of our Lord Jesus.

2.
What is the Mystery of Christ?

Romans 16:25–27

Now to him that is able to establish you according to my gospel and the preaching of Jesus Christ, according to the revelation of the mystery which hath been kept in silence through times eternal, but now is manifested, and by the scriptures of the prophets, according to the commandment of the eternal God, is made known unto all the nations unto obedience of faith: to the only wise God, through Jesus Christ, to whom be the glory for ever. Amen

Ephesians 3:2–13

if so be that ye have heard of the dispensation of that grace of God which was given me to you-ward; how that by revelation was made known unto me the mystery, as I wrote before in few words, whereby, when ye read, ye can perceive my understanding in the mystery of Christ; which in other generations was not made known unto the sons of men, as it hath now been revealed unto his holy apostles and prophets in the Spirit; [to wit], that the Gentiles are fellow-heirs, and

*fellow-members of the body,
and fellow-partakers of the
promise in Christ Jesus through
the gospel, whereof I was made
a minister, according to the
gift of that grace of God which
was given me according to the
working of his power. Unto me,
who am less than the least of
all saints, was this grace given,
to preach unto the Gentiles the
unsearchable riches of Christ;
and to make all men see what is
the dispensation of the mystery
which for ages hath been hid
in God who created all things;
to the intent that now unto the
principalities and the powers
in the heavenly [places] might
be made known through the
church the manifold wisdom of
God, according to the eternal
purpose which he purposed
in Christ Jesus our Lord: in
whom we have boldness and
access in confidence through
our faith in him. Wherefore I
ask that ye may not faint at my
tribulations for you, which are
your glory.*

Should we just bow once again in a short word of prayer? I always think when we deal with a matter like this one we are dealing with, we really need the illumination of the Holy Spirit. Let each one then just ask the Lord to really meet us.

Lord, when we come to this matter, which we believe to be so at the heart of everything in Thy Word, which Thou hast in Thy grace and sovereignty, vouchsafed Lord, to reveal to us, we pray, Lord, that we may not fall behind, in seeking such illumination, but rather, Lord, we may be pioneers, as it were, seeking Thy face day and night, that

*we might know this matter, not only Lord, in word, but in experience.
Now, Lord, wilt Thou give a special grace for this? Lord, we thank
Thee that we are here in Thy presence and Thou art able to meet with
us. Now release us from all the worries, cares, or exhaustion of the
day, Lord, and grant we pray that we may know the ministry of Thy
Spirit, to our bodies, to our souls, and above all, to our spirits. This we
ask in the name of our Lord Jesus, Amen.*

Now, we have begun to introduce this matter of the mystery
of Christ. This that we have read in the passage in Ephesians.
For instance, in verse four when the apostle said:

> *whereby, when you read, you can perceive my
> understanding in the mystery of Christ.*

Or again, in the words of the apostle Paul in Romans 16:25,
when he says:

> *... according to the revelation of the mystery, which
> has been kept in silence, through times eternal*

We have looked at the word *mystery* in our previous time.
I will just re-emphasize one thing about that. The common
usage today of the word *mystery* means: "a secret for which no
answer can be found and for which no explanation is adequate."
This is **not** the way the word is used in the Bible, especially in
the New Testament. It is not used as a secret, as some knowledge
withheld, but rather, of a secret which God wishes to communicate.

Always in connection with this marvellous word mystery, which is used a number of times, especially by the apostle Paul, we have the words: manifest, understand, received knowledge of, revelation of—everything is positive. It is not that it is withheld from us. Rather the emphasis is that it is communicated to us. The way we put it previously was that it is a secret revealed as a privilege to the initiated. That is how the word really is used in the New Testament. It is taken from those Greek mystery religions, where there were *initiates* into the mysteries—the mystery rites, the mystery sacraments and so on—associated with these things.

Now, the apostle Paul by the Holy Spirit, took this word and said, every born-again believer is a candidate for divine revelation. These matters which God for generations and ages has kept back, has kept secret, He has now revealed. He has communicated them to us. Now, I would have thought that if there was no other reason for seeking the Lord, it ought to be just that one fact. You have been born in an age and given, as it were, with your spiritual birthright, the privilege of understanding this mystery.

What is the Mystery?

Well, now I want to ask the question: "What is the mystery?" If you have your Bible with you, you will need it to really search out things. What is the mystery of Christ? It is quite clear that it has something to do with the eternal purpose of God. For instance, we read in Ephesians 3:9:

> ... to make all men see what is the dispensation of the mystery
> which for ages has been hid in God, who created all things

and verse 11:

> *according to the eternal purpose which He*
> *purposed in Christ Jesus, our Lord.*

So here is one thing. This matter which has been withheld, hid in God for ages, withheld from many, many successive generations, has something to do with the eternal purpose of God which He purposed in the Lord Jesus. There is another scripture in Ephesians 1:9:

> *making known unto us the mystery of His will according*
> *to His good pleasure which He purposed in Him*

that is in Jesus. So there again, it is something to do with this counsel of God, which He purposed in the Lord Jesus. There is the first thing to consider about this mystery.

Here is the second thing. It has something to do with being the body of the Messiah, with being the body of the Lord Jesus. We have this in Ephesians 3:10–11, the church:

> *to the intent, that now unto the principalities and the powers*
> *in the heavenly places might be made known through the*
> *church, the manifold wisdom of God, according to the*
> *eternal purpose which He purposed in Christ Jesus,*

Now in Ephesians 3:4–6 we are told:

> *... you can perceive my understanding in the mystery*

of Christ which in other generations not made known
unto the sons of men ... to wit, that the Gentiles are
fellow-heirs, and fellow-members of the body, and
fellow-partakers of the promise in Christ Jesus.

So here is a second clue. This mystery of Christ is to do with being fellow-members of the body, fellow-heirs, fellow-members, fellow-partakers. It has to do with fellowship, to do with sharing something, sharing Him, being the body of God's Messiah, being the body of the Lord Jesus, and being the church of God.

Here is a third thing that it seems this matter of mystery is linked with clearly. Ephesians 5:31–32:

For this cause shall a man leave his father and mother, and
shall cleave to his wife, and the two shall become one flesh. This
mystery is great, but I speak in regard of Christ and the church.

So here is the third thing: this mystery of Christ is to do with the bride of Christ, to do with the wife of the Lamb. Somehow, it is associated with those who are called to be His bride, His wife. That is the next thing.

Then lastly, in direct association anyway, it has to do with ultimate glory. Colossians 1:26–27:

even the mystery which had been hid for ages and
generations, but now hath it been manifested to His
saints, to whom God was pleased to make known what
is the riches of the glory of this mystery among the
Gentiles, which is Christ in you, the hope of glory.

Christ in you the hope of glory. We have the same thing in Ephesians 1:12. Remember again about that mystery which occurred just a few verses back in verse nine, "making known unto us the mystery of His will." Verse 12:

to the end, that we should be unto the praise of His glory.

Now, these are phrases which Christians tend to know: "the praise of His glory," "Christ in you, the hope of glory," "the body of Christ," "the church of God," "the bride of Christ," "the wife of the Lamb," "eternal purpose." I do not say that we understand them, but if you are a little acquainted with the Bible, and you have been a believer for at least two or three years, generally speaking, these are phrases which at least you know are biblical. They are Christian phrases. They are phrases to do with the gospel of God, with the whole counsel of God, but who understands them? It is one thing to know phrases. It is another thing to understand them. I mean, I know the word atom, but frankly, if you asked me to explain an atom, I think we would have some problem. You see, we can all know phrases, words, and terms, but when it comes to actually explaining what they mean we have only a vague, intuitive idea. To explain it, to give a reason for the hope that is within us, to be able to communicate it to somebody else, we could not do it. Yet this mystery, which was withheld from the patriarchs and the prophets and the kings and all those who have gone before has been granted as a privilege to every single born-again child of God in this dispensation. That ought to make us hungry for the Lord. It ought to make us really reach out to the Lord.

Let us just survey that again. This mystery of Christ has something to do with the eternal purpose of God, something to do with being members of the body of the Messiah, the church of God, something to do with being the bride of Christ, the wife of the Lamb, and something to do with ultimate glory, the final manifestation of the glory of God on the earth.

The Eternal Purpose of God

Now then, what is the mystery of Christ? Well, of course, now we really need the Lord's help. God had a plan, a purpose from the beginning, from before times eternal, right at the distant, distant, eternity, pre-time eternity, God had in His heart a plan, a purpose. And this purpose was centred in His Son. We know this because it says, "according to the eternal purpose, which He purposed in Christ Jesus our Lord."

Now, the Colossian letter puts it even more simply. Now let's read this very carefully. Speaking of the Lord Jesus in Colossians 1:15–17:

Who is the image of the invisible God,
the first-born of all creation.

That is the pattern of all creation, you understand, "the first-born of all, creation." Now it goes on:

For in Him were all things created in the heavens, and upon
the earth, things visible and things invisible, whether thrones
or dominions or principalities or powers, all things have
been created, through Him, and unto Him, and He is before

all things, and in Him, all things consist or hold together.

Now, I defy anybody to ever be able to fathom that. In my simple language (obviously not as full as this) what it is saying is this: that everything that has been created by God, visible and invisible, in heaven, and on earth, was created through the Lord Jesus. It was created not only through the Lord Jesus but for the Lord Jesus. Furthermore, He was before all these things. In other words, He was the pattern for it all. He was the basis for it all. He was the blueprint, if you like, for it all. He was before all things and in Him, it all holds together.

Now you might well ask, "Whatever has happened?" Here we are in a country that is anything but an illustration of that. We can hardly say that all this chaos on our little national level is through Him and for Him, that in Him it all holds together. Yet in some marvellous way, despite the fall, in spite of sin, in spite of the powers of darkness, everything that has been created (even though much has been usurped by the powers of darkness), has still been created through Him and for Him, and it is the very grace of God that holds the whole together now. God is waiting because once God has got the heart of the matter put right, then in the end He will work it out to the circumference. In the end, when He has got the heart of the matter right, He will work out from that to the far flung circumference until the whole is renewed and there is a new creation. As He said in the book of Revelation, "Behold, I make all things new." But first things first. Isn't it wonderful?

You know some people sometimes say to me, "Why did God not finish with it all?" Or, "Why did He not just wash His hands of it all?" Or, "Why did He not start again?" Well, He could have. There is no reason why God, when Adam and Eve failed, should not have said, "Alright. Blow them up. Finish with them. We will start all over again with a new world, no sin, and we will go on until we get a perfect couple. Then each time anything goes wrong, we will blow them up." But I am not sure that would reveal the heart of God, or the love of God, or the patience of God, or the faithfulness of God, or the kind of person God is. You know, His enduring patience, His steadfast patience and love over a world that has gone hopelessly askew is really wonderful. Think how in the end He is going to do something that is going to be the marvel of all the ages to come. I know it is speculation, but I can't help but imagine that far, far out in space, there must be other inhabited universes. I sometimes think to myself that perhaps they never fell. They actually did, in fact, partake of the tree of life. However, if that is so (and there is an if) then there is no single universe amongst all those innumerable universes that will be more precious or more marvelled at than the one universe that went astray—and God brought back.

Now, let's get back to this again. God had a plan, a purpose from the beginning, centred in His Son. Let's look at another scripture that may help. You see, all these scriptures are what we call "deep" scriptures. You start reading these and people say, "Oh! You know we really are under ...!" No. If you had a few of the saints who were saved on the day of Pentecost with you, quite unlettered people, they probably would tell you that they understood these things from the beginning—perfectly simple. Yet we tend to feel that once you know something about forgiveness and being saved and cleansing then that is the simple gospel. If anything goes beyond that, you begin to get out of your depth. And psychologically, we flounder the moment we start to hear anything else, but it is not so.

Now let's read Hebrews 1:2. I will have to start with the phrase of the first verse:

God hath at the end of these days spoken unto us
in [His] Son, whom He appointed heir of all things,
through whom also He made the worlds.

Whom He appointed heir of all things. So the Son is the heir of all things. He is the genuine heir. Satan has said that he will inherit, he will take the place of the Son of God, he will be like the Most High, but the Lord Jesus is the true heir of all things. Now, that is the first thing about this matter of the mystery. It has something to do with a purpose which was in God's heart right back in the pre-time eternity, through which and by which He created the universe and everything that is in it. He created mankind in His image. It is centred in His Son.

In Christ

Now, here is the second thing. If you want something to get hold of, this little phrase is the key to the mystery of Christ. It comes again and again and again in the New Testament. It is the simplest way that one can communicate the mystery of Christ: *in Christ*. It explains everything: in Christ. You see, the whole is explained. It is the key to the whole matter, to this mystery, because God had a purpose in Christ. Then through Christ He starts to save a people and He brings them into Christ. Then He begins to form them in Christ and then from that people, He begins to go out to bring a whole creation back into Christ.

Let's have a further look at this. Now this phrase again, this eternal purpose, Ephesians 3:11:

according to the eternal purpose which He
purposed in Christ Jesus our Lord.

As we mentioned already, in the New American Standard Bible, it says, "according to the eternal purpose which He carried out in Christ Jesus our Lord." Carried out in Christ Jesus; I like that. The Revised Standard Version puts it also very lucidly. It says, "according to the eternal purpose, which He realised in Christ Jesus our Lord." So it is not only purposed, it is carried out. It was not only that God had a purpose centred in His Son, He has carried out that purpose in His Son. Now we are coming home on this topic, I hope.

You see if we begin to think about how it has been carried out in His Son, well, what about the gospels? We have four gospels. Somewhere there we must have what He carried out in His Son. If it has been realised in His Son, then somewhere in these four gospels, we should be able to discover what it is that He has "realised in His Son"—so we have no excuse. Once we get hold of the matter, then we should be able to go back to the Old Testament prophets and find that they all spoke about this matter. Then we would go on into the letters of Paul and find that we have a tremendous exposition of this whole matter. It becomes so exciting! People say they find the Bible boring. Well, of course, you will find it boring if you keep to a kind of mundane diet.

If you don't really start to ask God for illumination and start to move out of the shallow waters that you are in. You want to launch out! Get out of what you have known up to now and start saying, "Lord, there is more, there is more! I want to know what it is. I want to launch out into this. I want to be a Christian with the whole counsel of God, not just a simple gospel!"

This word *simple gospel* never comes anywhere in the whole Bible! People say, "You know, I preach the simple gospel." Well, they don't preach the gospel the apostle Paul or the apostles preached! They preached the whole gospel, the whole counsel of God. The apostle Paul was very, very fiery on this point. He said, "You know, I have given you the whole counsel of God. You have been witnesses to it. I did not withhold anything from you, I gave you the whole thing, although you may not have understood it." I don't think for a single moment that the church in Ephesus could have ever understood the Ephesian letter since all of us have had such a hard time with it. They must have also sort-of said, "What is he talking about?"

We will never understand these things unless we have a seeking heart. The whole point of a time like this, a series like this is to inflame your appetite. It is to sort of give you (I know I should not say this) a sherry to get your appetite going. A spiritual sherry, I mean, to give you some kind of something that sort of gets all the taste buds excited. So that from now on you say, I can't be bothered with all that is less. I've got something more. There is something more in this book. There is something more in God for me and I must have it. I must know it!"

Today, the whole realm for youngsters is pop-style gospel music! Personally, I haven't anything against pop-style gospel music, yet I know some others … they would tear you limb from limb. But I don't have too much against pop-style gospel music if you want to play that kind of thing. I mean, fancy, you think you've been saved just to listen endlessly to pop-style gospel music on and on, day after day, night after night and that's the gospel? I'm not saying that you want to listen to Handel's *Messiah* day and night, or some Bach cantata or Mendelssohn's *Elijah*. I'm not asking you to be all classical. But what I am asking is this: do you see that this gospel has something special? The apostle speaks of this gospel as being a revelation according to the mystery which God has revealed to us. This gospel is according to the mystery which He has revealed to us. I don't think most Christians' appreciation of the gospel is according to the mystery which has been revealed. It is much, much less than that. So you see, this is rather wonderful when we look at it.

A Home for God

Now let's get back to the point. This eternal purpose, this purpose that has been in God's heart from pre-time eternity, has been carried out in the Lord Jesus. It has been realised in the Lord Jesus. Well, now what on earth does this mean? Simply this: God has found His home in Christ. It is as simple as that. God has found His home on Earth, in Christ.

Now, think for a moment about this matter. Genesis 1:2 says that the Spirit of God, hovered, brooded upon the face of the deep and everything was without form. Everything was void. Then God began. "Let there be light," He said, and there was light. Then He said something else about the firmament, heaven being divided from the earth, and then day and night, and so on and so on. But the beginning was this: the Spirit of God brooded on the face of the deep. It was as if the Holy Spirit was brooding over the whole earth—looking, may I put it, as a dove for a home.

Do you remember the beautiful story, the history of Noah? Do you remember at the end of the flood when he let out a raven? It did not come back. Ravens are very shrewd birds. They are also unclean birds. Of course, he did not come back! He found some floating dead carrion, sat on it and had a wonderful meal. Then Noah woke up and thought, "Oh, I was silly to let that bird out. I will let out a dove." Now a dove will not touch anything dead and the dove flew around trying to find a place to rest but found none and came back with a twig in its mouth. Do you remember?

Now, you know, to me this is like a picture of the Holy Spirit. You see when He was looking over that whole face of the deep—formless, void—it was as if the Holy Spirit was saying, "Where is the home? Where is God's home? Where is His resting place? Where is that in which He can come home to be Himself"? Well, I know this is speaking of God in very, sort of Sunday school terms, but we have to. We cannot understand it any other way. Out of that formless void, God created something, but there was no rest for the Holy Spirit. God said it is good! It is all good! But there was no rest for God because God does not dwell in natural creation. He does not dwell in houses of bricks and mortar or stone. He does not dwell in organisations or systems or philosophies. God dwells in human beings. That is His plan. That is His purpose—to come home into human beings, to find His home in the men and women that He created—but He found none. All the way through the record of the Old Testament, the Holy Spirit never came home. Only twice do you find that the glory of God filled something, and there was the smoke of His presence which even the priest could not go into. Do you remember where it was? In Exodus 40, the last verses to do with the erection of the tabernacle. You will remember the moment that the tabernacle was erected according to the plan, which God gave of heavenly things, then that moment, the whole was filled with the presence of His glory. You will remember the second time is in II Chronicles 7:1–3. It was when the temple was dedicated after it was built. You will remember the presence of God's glory came into the whole and filled it so that the priests could not stand to minister and all the people bowed with their heads to the ground and worshipped.

Now, that tabernacle and that temple was only a figure, or a type, a symbol, a Sunday school picture, if you like, of the real thing, and even in the little picture—God could not hold Himself back, if you see what I mean. God knew very well He does not dwell in tabernacles made by men, He does not dwell in temples, or houses that men have made either in the Old or the New Covenant. But that was a picture. It was in the time when God was doing everything in picture form, in type form, you understand. So even with the tabernacle, it was as if God said, "Oh, I have waited, I have waited, I have waited from pre-time eternity for this! This is only the figure, but I will fill the whole thing with my glory, and not one of those priests will even be able to come near. I want to show them, this is what is on my heart!" Exactly the same happened with the temple.

However, you will never find God resting at home anywhere else—until Jesus. Of course, you know what happened when Jesus was born in Bethlehem. I don't have to tell you that, but you must surely know what happened when He went down to be baptised in the river Jordan. You will find it in the gospel of Mark 1:9–11:

> *And it came to pass in those days, that Jesus came from Nazareth of Galilee, and was baptised of John in the Jordan. And straightway coming up out of the water, He saw the heavens rent asunder, and the Spirit as a dove descending upon him: and a voice came out of the heavens, 'Thou art My beloved Son, in Thee I am well pleased.'*

Now in John 1, John the Baptist said, that He upon whom the Holy Spirit comes and remains, is He that God has spoken to him of. Do you remember? What does it mean? It means that the Spirit of God, after all those thousands of years of human history, had come home. For the first time, the Holy Spirit found a man, as a man, apart from His Godhead, found a man Jesus, who was absolutely without sin, and absolutely holy, and absolutely according to the mind of God—and in that moment, He came to rest and the heavens opened. The heavens could never be opened on the other kind of man, from Adam to Jesus. Because we were all fallen, all sinful, all had fallen short of the glory of God. But upon Jesus, the heavens opened and God said, "Thou art My well beloved Son, in Thee I am well pleased."

Now even more remarkable is the little thing that John says in John 1:49–51. You will all know the story, those of you who know your Bibles:

> *Nathanael answered him, Rabbi, thou art the Son of God; thou art the King of Israel, Jesus answered and said unto*

him, Because I said unto thee, I saw thee underneath a
fig tree, believest thou? thou shalt see greater things than
these. And he saith unto him, Verily, verily I say unto
you, Ye shall see the heaven open, and the angels of God
ascending and descending upon the Son of Man.

Now, what do you think this means? I do not know how well you know your Bible, but you see when Jesus said earlier, "Here is an Israelite, in whom there is no guile," He used the word "Jacob." Here is an Israelite, in whom there is no *Jacob*! Later on, when He said, "Did you believe that I am the Son of God, the King of Israel because I said, I saw you under a fig tree? You shall see greater things than these. What shall you see? You should see heaven open and the angels of God ascending and descending on the Son of Man." He was referring to the dream of Jacob in Genesis 28:12–19. Do you remember that dream that God gave Jacob, and he saw a ladder stretching from the earth into heaven? He saw angels descending and ascending—a little different. Then he said, this is none other than what? "This is none other than the house of God." *Bet El*—the house of God.

What does it mean? It means this: that Jesus is God's home! For the first time God has got His home on earth! He has found the person in whom He can come absolutely home. Not a lodging place, not a hotel, not an inn—but home! That is why John the Baptist was told: "The One upon whom you see the Holy Spirit descending and abiding, He is the Messiah."

God had come home! He had not come like He did upon Saul, just to prophesy for a little while or upon some of the others to do great and skilful work. He had not come like He did upon Samson that He might exercise tremendous supernatural strength, or as upon some of the others that they might fulfil some point in God's economy. He came upon Jesus, that He might dwell there forever.

This is exactly what the Lord Jesus said in John 2:19–22:

> *Jesus answered and said unto them, Destroy this temple, and in three days I will raise it up. The Jews therefore said, Forty and six years was this temple in building, and wilt Thou raise it up in three days? But He spake of the temple of His body. When therefore He was raised from the dead, His disciples remembered that He spake this; and they believed the scripture, and the word that Jesus had said.*

Now, I do not think that we should just think of it simply as a reference to the personal body of the Lord Jesus just being crucified, buried, and raised. Jesus said, "this body, this being of mine, is the temple of God. It is the house of God. Destroy it and in three days I will raise it up." Now listen, you are very near to an understanding of the mystery of Christ. If you followed this, even very, very weakly up to this point, if you can take the next step—you are there.

Remain

"In three days, I will raise it up." Through His finished work on the cross—His death, His burial, and resurrection—all who are saved are in Him. Are you saved? You say, "Yes." How were you saved? You say, "Through the finished work of the Lord Jesus on the cross." Yes, through His death, burial and resurrection. Where are you now? Well, now you begin to quake a little, "Well, I'm following the Lord." Yes, yes, yes, I know that. "Well, I'm seeking to be obedient." Yes, yes, yes, but where are you? Are you in Adam or are you in Christ? Are you in the first man or are you in the second Man? Are you in the old man or are you in the new man? Are you in the old creation or are you in the new creation? Now do you begin to get it? If you have been saved, you are in Him.

Now we begin to see something tremendous, we begin to see now, thank God, if we are in Him, we are in the home of God! We have come into the home of God. Well, it should make you dance with joy! Even at a miserable time—strike-ridden, a world falling to pieces and I do not know what else—yet this is what God has done for us. He has brought us to the place where we are in His Son, and if we are in His Son, then we are in the house of God. We are in the home of God.

Now, just wait; let us understand this a little more. What did the Lord Jesus say in one of the very last messages He gave? It is recorded in John 15. It was given after the Passover Feast somewhere between that upper room and Gethsemane. Do you remember? "I am the true vine. My Father is the husbandman." Then He went on and said, "Abide in Me and I in you." That word *abide* is beautiful. He did not say, "Fight to get in me, and I will fight to get in you. Strive to get into me, and I will strive to get into you." He did not even say more graciously, "Strive to get into Me, and I will graciously abide in you." He said, "Abide in Me and I in you." Abide is really *remain*. You cannot remain if you are not already there. Do you understand? How can you stay, if you are not already there in the place? If I say, "Remain in the library." You must already be in the library. If I say to you, "Go to the library and remain." That is different, but if I say, "Abide in the library," it means you are already in the library. Do you understand? So here we have something simply wonderful. The Lord Jesus said, "I am the true vine. I am the vine, you are the branches." Somehow or other, you are in! "You are part of Me. You come home to Me. You and I, we share one life! Now abide in Me and I in you."

You have the same thing in this matter of the temple. You know the word of God so well, but perhaps after what I have said to you,it may come home to you with new force. Now, you know these words, so don't let them run off you like water off a duck's back, really listen. Ephesians 2:20–22:

> *Being built upon the foundation of the apostles and*
> *prophets, Christ Jesus himself being the chief corner stone,*
> *in whom each several building, fitly framed together,*
> *groweth into a holy temple in the Lord; in whom ye also*
> *are builded together for a habitation of God in the Spirit.*

Remain Where?

Did you notice in whom, in whom, in whom? *In the Lord Jesus,* the whole building fitly framed together groweth into a holy temple in the Lord. You could not get it more clearly, could you? It did not say a holy temple *of* the Lord; it is the holy temple *in* the Lord. You have got it twice! In whom? *In* the Lord. In whom you are builded together—as a habitation of God in the Spirit. Now, you see, I say that this is simply tremendous. This is the mystery of Christ.

Let me take it one little bit further. Because we have been saved through the finished work of the Lord Jesus through His death, burial, and resurrection when He was raised as the temple of God, He has become the chief cornerstone, and we, as living stones, are built together upon that foundation, and grow into a holy temple in the Lord. What a marvellous privilege is yours and mine to share with the Lord Jesus like this!

Ah, there is something more. We have become part of Him. I do not mean to devalue His essential deity, but we have become partakers of the divine nature. The apostle Peter says so in II Peter 1:4: we have become partakers of the divine nature. In the most wonderful ways, the Russian liturgy so beautifully puts it:

God became man, in order that man might become part of God.

We cannot take it too far, but it is true. We become partakers of the divine nature, we become part of Him, we become members of His body.

So essential is this union, so organic, so lively, and so vital that it is just like fingers and hands and feet and toes and legs and muscles and all the different parts of a human body. We are not members on a membership role, I cannot think of anything more deadly—all our little names in serried ranks [close rows] on some dusty old piece of paper in some archive in some vestry. No! We are living members, we are limbs of Christ, parts of Him.

Now we must not take it too far, but isn't it wonderful? I find it simply marvellous. No wonder the apostle Paul said, "You can perceive my understanding in the mystery" (see Ephesians 3:4). He was just overboard about it. "Oh, I've been called to preach the unsearchable riches of Christ to the Gentiles." To that lot? Let them hear all of it, bring them into it. Why? Because this mystery is this: what God began in the Jewish people has to go to the ends of the earth and from every kindred, tongue, people, and nation will come those who will become part of what God began in the Jewish people and will end with the Jewish people. That is why.

What is this mystery? Listen to it, "You shall perceive my understanding of this mystery of Christ." What is it? It is this: "You are fellow-heirs, fellow-members of the body." Fellow members with whom? With the saved Jews, going right back to Abraham. Did the Lord Jesus not say this? "There shall come a day when they shall come from the west and from the south and from the north and from the east and they shall sit down in the kingdom of God with Abraham, with Isaac, and with Jacob."

Then people immediately say to me, "Yes, but just wait! The Lord Himself said the least in the kingdom of God is greater than John the Baptist." Quite right—in privilege. Get that clear. It does not mean for one single moment that John the Baptist is of less spiritual character than most of us. He is a giant spiritually! This is a disgraceful teaching that has gone round that Abraham and Isaac are all pitiful little characters because they were under the Old Covenant. I have never heard such nonsense because when you come to the City, you find there are 12 foundations and 12 gates, the 12 apostles and the 12 tribes, the patriarchs. No, no, no. Now here is your responsibility. John the Baptist did not have one-tenth of the privileges that are yours, not one-tenth. I would go further. He had not even one percent of the privileges that are yours. You have the gospel law written on your heart. You have the Holy Spirit given to you. You have all the mysteries unveiled to you! John the Baptist had none of them, nor did any of the others, yet they overcame. It says in Hebrews 11, "... and have become inheritors of the promise." Dear friends, this should shake us up. Do you think that God is going to be pleased that He has scattered these privileges, poured them out upon us and we have squandered them? No, not at all.

Now come back to this matter. You see it is really very wonderful; we have become part of the Lord Jesus. This is our privilege. This is the mystery of Christ hid from other ages and generations now made known to us: that we are members of the Messiah. Oh, those others longed for the Messiah, they looked for the Messiah, they saw Him as some divine figure that would come to the people of God and would bring righteousness and salvation and deliverance, and set up the kingdom of God and the throne of God. But it was never revealed to them that those whom the Messiah would save would become an integral part of Himself. That was hid, but not to you. You may be the most unworthy child in the kingdom of God, but to you, this mystery has been communicated.

The Bride of Christ

This is what it means when it says that we are to be His bride, that we are to be His wife. I have read Ephesians 5:31–32:

> For this cause shall a man leave his father and
> mother, and shall cleave to his wife; and the two
> shall become one flesh. This mystery is great: but I
> speak in regard of Christ and of the church.

When we read the whole of this passage about husbands and wives, we suddenly find that the apostle Paul has really got Christ and the church behind the whole thing. He says, "this mystery being so great."

Now, I know it is no longer fashionable in these days of women's lib to speak of Genesis 2 and the way that the woman was created. But women's lib, or no women's lib, we cannot get over the word of God and the word of God is this: that God brought all the animals from the creation before Adam, yet God did not name them. He stood aside and let Adam name them. I find that very interesting. Why did God not say, "Now this animal coming up is an elephant. Elephant, Adam. This now coming up is a giraffe. Giraffe, Adam" and Adam would say, "Giraffe." What was the Lord doing? The Lord never named them. It was as if He were saying, "Adam, I have created you without sin, but you are not complete. I want to bring this incompleteness out of you. I want to see if there is any one of these animals that you feel you could settle down with."

Now, that may seem very disgusting to you, but I mean, even the ape when it went by after all that, Adam might have said, "Ooh, well, I mean it is the nearest to me." Even the orangutan, as it went by, Adam said, "No no, Lord. We will call that an orangutan," and said, "Goodbye," to the orangutan. Then it says, "There was no helpmeet for him." But here in the Hebrew, it is very beautiful: "There was nothing that answered him." Nothing that answered—that is the key to it. There was not one of those animals that answered him. He could keep them as pets, he could admire them, he could marvel at them, he could see the glory of God's creation in them, but they did not answer to him. Then God put him to sleep, opened his side, took out flesh and bone, and created woman, and closed his side. Then man awakened, and God said, "Now what about this, Adam?" And Adam said, "Oh, this is me." His name was *Ish* in Hebrew, but he called her, *Isha*, "me again." It is me again! Not me—and yet me. The opposite end of me, the other side of me, the other half of me. Do you understand? Are you getting it?

That was the first Adam. What did God do with the last Adam? God put him to sleep on the cross and in that moment, in John chapter 19:30, it says that He cried with a loud voice and He said, "It is finished" and in that moment, the veil of the temple was torn in two, from top to bottom, the whole thing was finished. The work of our salvation was completed, there was nothing to be added, not one jot, not one tittle was to be added. God had done it, He had accomplished it. It was finished. "And then," says John, "a soldier went up to Him and pierced His side and forthwith there came out blood and water." Then he says, "He that bore witness, his witness is true." Why does he make so much about this? "Oh you see, of course, you see, that was salvation!" No, no friend, it was not salvation. The salvation had been completed in the finished work. What then was that opening of His side? We get it in 1 John 5:4–12. I wonder whether you have ever connected these words with this matter. They are very mysterious words, from verse four:

> *For whatsoever is begotten of God overcometh the world: and this is the victory that hath overcome the world, [even] our faith. And who is he that overcometh the world, but he that believeth that Jesus is the Son of God? This is he that came by water and blood, [even] Jesus Christ; not with the water only,*

but with the water and with the blood. And it is the Spirit
that beareth witness, because the Spirit is the truth. For there
are three who bear witness, the Spirit, and the water, and the
blood: and the three agree in one. If we receive the witness of
men, the witness of God is greater: for the witness of God is
this, that he hath borne witness concerning his Son. He that
believeth on the Son of God hath the witness in him: he that
believeth not God hath made him a liar; because he hath not
believed in the witness that God hath borne concerning his
Son. And the witness is this, that God gave unto us eternal
life, and this life is in his Son. He that hath the Son hath
the life; he that hath not the Son of God hath not the life.

Now, here is the wonderful thing. When God put Jesus to sleep, He opened His side, and by blood and water through the work of the Holy Spirit, He created a woman so that every single child of God born of the Spirit comes by water and by blood. Life! That is the meaning of the church. The church is not a theology. It is not a theory. It is not an ideal. It is not an organisation. It is not a social club. It is not some friendship society. What is the church? Is it just a place where lonely people can meet each other? No, no, no. Those things may all be entailed in it, included in it, but that is not the church. The church is Jesus. The church is the nature and life of Jesus, created by the Holy Spirit in others so that suddenly we belong to Him. We are created out of Him. We have become part of the new creation, part of the new man. He is the head, we are the body. He is the husband; we are the wife. He is the bridegroom; we are the bride. Do you begin to understand?

I will put it very simply like this: we have been incorporated. Literally, incorporated. I do not mean it in a business way. I mean in this way: we have been made the body of the Lord Jesus. Now, we know that from Colossians 1:18, where it says:

And He is the head of the body, which is the church.

Or I think of other wonderful scriptures, like in Romans 12:5:

*... although there be many members, yet
are we one body in Christ.*

This is marvellous when we begin to see it. 1 Corinthians 12:12, says:

... though there be many members, yet, is there one Christ.

They are all in Him.

Ultimate Glory

Now, this union with Christ is so tremendous. It is a matter of glory. That bride is also the city of God, do you all know that? No one ever speaks of his wife as his city. It would seem a very strange thing, if you said, "Come on, City. We will go home now." But the Bible says that this bride is the city. We have it in Revelation 21, where again and again we are told about the bride, the wife of the Lamb, the New Jerusalem, the Holy City. If you look very carefully at these scriptures showing that city in Revelation 21:10–11:

coming down out of out of heaven ... having the glory of God.

Or I think of 1 Peter 5:10–11:

The God of all grace, who has called you unto His eternal glory.

Where? In Christ Jesus. Called unto His eternal glory in Christ Jesus. You have been called to share the glory of God in the Lord Jesus. What a calling!

Well, I think of another wonderful scripture that we have quoted once or twice, "... the riches of the glory of this mystery among the Gentiles, which is Christ in you the hope of glory." Now, do you not think when you begin to really get this that it becomes very exciting? For instance, I think of these wonderful words in Romans 9:23, 24:

and that he might make known the riches of his
glory upon vessels of mercy, which he afore prepared
unto glory, [even] us, whom he also called, not from
the Jews only, but also from the Gentiles?

Isn't this wonderful? I thank God that He gave me some revelation of this mystery! The little that I see of it, it just thrills me. It has kept me going all through these years. I find it so exciting! No wonder the apostles went overboard on this, as if they could not contain themselves. This is so exciting, so tremendous. Now, if it is a matter of sharing the glory of the Lord Jesus, it is a matter of coming to the throne of God.

What is a city? A bride speaks of something intimate, secret, personal, direct, union, communion. What is a city? it is the centre of administration, a place of public intercourse, it is a place where matters get settled and done, and policies are worked out and fulfilled. You have two things. We are called to share the glory of the Lord Jesus not only as His wife, as His bride in the most intimate, direct, personal way, but we are called to come to the throne with Him and share in His reign. Not just marvel at His reign, but be involved in His government. Now if that is so, I begin to understand a whole lot of other things. I understand what he said in Romans 8:17:

> and if children, then heirs; heirs of God, and joint-heirs with Christ; if so be that we suffer with him, that we may be also glorified with him.

Or I think of those words of the Lord Jesus, in Revelation 3:21:

> He that overcometh, I will give to him to sit down with me in my throne, as I also overcame, and sat down with my Father in his throne.

Well, dear ones, you see, a matter like this cannot take just a few moments, can it? Now, listen carefully because there are some heresies on this and I want to be very careful. It is for this revealing of the sons of God that the whole natural creation longingly awaits. Did you hear that? It is for this revealing of the sons of God. Get it right. Not the *children* of God, the *sons* of God. Oh, but you say "You cannot make a distinction between children and sons." No, in one way, but yes, in another. We are all sons of God through faith, but a babe cannot sit on a throne and reign, practically. A babe, a child cannot take over a family business or the family estates, can it? You know, a father may say, "So-and-so is my child," but when the child has grown up to full discretion and maturity, I have never heard a father say, "So-and-so is my *child.*" He says, "So-and-so is my *son.*" Now when that son was a baby, he was still a son, wasn't he? Do you understand? When he was a baby, he was still a son. So of course, it is quite right. He was a son all the way through. But sometimes the Spirit of God uses this word son to speak of some maturity, some growth, a reaching of a certain point of growth. This is what the Scripture refers to as *perfection*, which is very unfortunately misunderstood in some quarters. I like the word *maturity* much better.

You see, if you look at Romans 8, we have just read that verse 17, "joint-heirs, heirs of God, joint-heirs with Christ," then listen to verses 18–19:

> *For I reckon that the sufferings of this present time are*
> *not worthy to be compared with the glory which shall be*
> *revealed to us-ward. For the earnest expectation of the*
> *creation waiteth for the revealing of the sons of God.*

The New American Standard Bible puts it even more clearly:

> *For I consider that the sufferings of this present time are not*
> *worthy to be compared with the glory that is to be revealed*
> *to us. For the anxious longing of the creation waits eagerly,*
> *for the revealing of the sons of God. For the creation was*

subjected to futility, not of its own will, but because of him
who subjected it in hope, that the creation itself also will
be set free from its slavery to corruption, into the freedom
of the glory of the children of God (Romans 8:18–21).

That is the whole! Now listen:

For we know that the whole creation groans and
suffers the pains of childbirth together until now. And
not only this but also we ourselves having the first
fruits of the Spirit, even we ourselves groan within
ourselves, waiting eagerly for our adoption as sons,
the redemption of our body (Romans 8:22–23).

The revealing of the sons ... What does this mean? Very simply, there is a sense in which that long awaited day cannot come unless the Lord has the required number for His eternal government. Did you hear? Do you think God is so stupid, so senseless, that He who has created a brain and given us intelligence would do something quite opposite? I cannot always say that it is true of us, but it ought to be so that we are always looking ahead. We are seeing that within a year or two, this-and-this is going to happen, and unless we are prepared for it, we are going to be undone. God gave us brains; God gave us intelligence. God gave us a kind of ability to at least weigh out the pros and the cons of a situation to understand it a bit. Do you mean to tell me that God is going to willy-nilly bring the day in when He has not got those people who can form an administration in the new heaven and the new earth? Wouldn't that be just to start the whole cycle all over again?

No, that is why it says, the natural creation waits for the revealing of the sons of God, these are not just children, these are children that have grown up. This is the mystery of Christ.

We shall go on and we shall now begin to talk about it more in the whole matter of the practical side. God does not give light so that we may compromise, that we might contradict it in practice. If God reveals a matter like this mystery to us, it is that you and I might have the obedience of faith. Did you hear those words in Romans 16:25–26 with which we began? We will end with them. Listen again and may God bring you to this place.

> *Now to Him that is able to establish you according to my*
> *gospel, and the preaching of Jesus Christ, according to the*
> *revelation of the mystery which had been kept in silence through*
> *times eternal, but now is manifested, and by the scriptures of*
> *the prophets, according to the commandments of the eternal*
> *God is made known unto us for the obedience of faith ...*

For what? For the obedience of faith. That is why God sometimes does not communicate this mystery to some people. There is no obedience of faith. God never cast pearls before swine lest they turn and trample it under foot; lest they take it and say, "Hmmph! Pressure of circumstances? We will do this and this," and contradict the light God has given us. That is why there is such a scarcity and a dearth of vision in our days. Obedience—we live in days of disobedience, days of anarchy, days of disorder, days of strife, and days of rebellion—it makes no difference. This mystery is communicated for the obedience of faith. May God give to you that obedience of faith.

Trust and obey,
For there's no other way,
To be happy in Jesus,
But to trust and obey.

Then these things which are so tremendous will become simplicity itself to you. They will become your flesh and blood. They will come to mean to you more than life itself. It will be the very meaning of your existence, the call, the very destiny that God has predetermined for you. May the Lord help you in this matter. Shall we pray?

Now, Lord, we do pray that Thou will not allow this to be wasted, not in any single part. We pray, Lord, that Thou will take these poor words of mine, and Thou wilt make them become a vehicle of communication for divine illumination and enlightenment to all of us. Lord, grant us that obedience of faith. Give us that humility of spirit and heart that bows before Thee Lord, that begins to seek Thee, that recognises its lack of wisdom, and asks Thee for that wisdom, which is from above, which Thou dost give liberally, and over which Thou dost not upbraid. Lord, we pray that since it has been our privilege to have this mystery revealed to us, we may become the true recipients of all this light. That light may shine into us corporately, shine into each of our lives, shine into our homes, transforming us Lord, so that we shall see our light affliction, which is but for a moment, which worketh for us an exceeding and eternal weight of glory. And this we ask, in the name of our Lord Jesus. Amen.

3.
The Challenge

Romans 16:25–27

Now to him that is able to establish you according to my gospel and the preaching of Jesus Christ, according to the revelation of the mystery which hath been kept in silence through times eternal, but now is manifested, and by the scriptures of the prophets, according to the commandment of the eternal God, is made known unto all the nations unto obedience of faith: to the only wise God, through Jesus Christ, to whom be the glory for ever. Amen.

Ephesians 3:2–12

... if so be that ye have heard of the dispensation of that grace of God which was given me to you-ward; how that by revelation was made known unto me the mystery, as I wrote before in few words, whereby, when ye read, ye can perceive my understanding in the mystery of Christ; which in other generations was not made known unto the sons of men, as it hath now been revealed unto his holy apostles and prophets in the Spirit; [to wit], that the Gentiles are fellow-heirs, and

fellow-members of the body, and fellow-partakers of the promise in Christ Jesus through the gospel, whereof I was made a minister, according to the gift of that grace of God which was given me according to the working of his power. Unto me, who am less than the least of all saints, was this grace given, to preach unto the Gentiles the unsearchable riches of Christ; and to make all men see what is the dispensation of the mystery which for ages hath been hid in God who created all things; to the intent that now unto the principalities and the powers in the heavenly [places] might be made known through the church the manifold wisdom of God, according to the eternal purpose which he purposed in Christ Jesus our Lord: in whom we have boldness and access in confidence through our faith in him.

As you know, we have been talking about this phrase: *the mystery of Christ.* Remember this word mystery is used in a very especial way in the New Testament and does not mean what we normally mean by the word mystery in the common usage of the English word. You know, generally, by using the word mystery, we mean some secret which is withheld, but in the Bible this Greek word means the exact opposite. It is a secret which is communicated only to those who are initiated. In other words, the accent is upon the grace of God, in bringing those who are born of God into a glorious understanding of a secret. This secret which has been hid all the way through the generations, but which now He has manifested or revealed or communicated. Now if we understand that, it starts to open us up quite considerably on this matter.

Really the essential key is the two little words *in Christ*. That is the key to this mystery. It is the glorious fact that not only was God *in Christ* reconciling the world, but that the Lord Jesus became the home of God on earth for the first time. Not the lodging place of God just passing through, not just a place where God just visited, but He became the home of God, the house of God. That is why Jesus said, "Destroy this temple, and in three days I will raise it up." He spoke of the temple of His body. When He was raised up on the third day, He became the chief cornerstone of a building of which God is the builder. The apostle Paul says in Ephesians 2:21,22:

We shall grow into a holy temple in the Lord, builded together as a habitation [or a home] *of God in the Spirit."*

Now, what we have said in the previous chapter is the heart of the matter. All we have got to say about the practical relevance of it and the challenge of it, really hasn't got the same depth of meaning if you do not get hold of what this mystery really is. Since you are a child of God and born of the Spirit, what a privilege it is that God has given to you: this which was hidden for ages and generations has now been communicated. It is something into which every one of us has to be brought.

Now, I want to speak on the challenge inherent within the *revelation* of the mystery of Christ. What is the challenge that is inherent, not within the mystery, but what is the challenge that is inherent within the revelation of the mystery? God does not cast pearls before swine. If He knows that you are just going to trample over this, God will not reveal it to you. However, wherever He finds a meek heart, and a heart that is ready to obey, and a heart that is ready to go on with Him, then He will start to really reveal it.

Divine Light is Essential

Now, divine light, once granted, cannot be compromised or contradicted in practice without incurring the most grave consequences. I wonder whether that sunk in to you all. Divine light, once granted, cannot be compromised or contradicted in practice without incurring the most grave consequences. Now, I do wish this could get into your hearts. I know that there are times when I tend to speak rather forcefully and sometimes perhaps, inadvisedly. But the burden on my heart has been this simple thing: that when God gives us light, the enemy will do every single thing in his power to pressurise us, both leadership and people, into contradicting it. No one is so foolish as to think that light will ever be contradicted blatantly. No one who knows the Lord ever contradicts the light of God blatantly; it always comes through the back door. It always comes through the pressure of circumstances. Things become difficult and things become pressurised. We begin to work, the problems mount up, and we wonder what we can do here, there and everywhere. Before we know where we are, we take action or we change things. Sometimes it may seem to be just a detail, but suddenly, something that God has given to us has been compromised.

The whole problem of divine light is this: once we compromise, it is the "thin end of the wedge." Let us be quite honest about this. We only have to look at the whole of church history. There is not a single movement of the Holy Spirit in the long history of the church, of the people of God, which has not gone off the rails at some point. Each of these instances has begun with some small excess, some small extreme. Somehow or other some action has been taken which has become the thin end of the wedge. That is why *light* is a tremendously important matter. It is why the Charismatic Movement has, with its emphasis upon life, quite rightly, come into grave danger by not at the same time emphasising the essential nature of *light*. Life and light go together. It is an interesting thing, as I have said before, that light precedes life in John's great epistle. When he speaks of God as light, he then speaks of God as love and then speaks of God as life.

Light preceded life. God said, "Let there be light," and there was light. Then God said, "Let the earth be caused to bring forth," and it came forth, and "let the waters team with teaming things," and let there be flying things in the heavens and so on and so forth. Light came first—life followed. Now it will be a fine theological point to decide which really comes first: life or light, but it is interesting that, at least in this whole matter of unfolding it to us, God puts light first, and life comes second. Is that not how you and I were born of God? Didn't a shaft of divine light shine into our hearts and in that moment we responded to God and became alive unto God through the work of the Holy Spirit? These two things then go hand in hand. You see, the whole challenge that is inherent within the revelation of the mystery of Christ is that once the light of God shines into our hearts and we begin to see what the mystery really is—the privilege of it, the glory of it, the wonder of it, the dynamic of it—then we have to be very careful that we do not compromise on what God has shown us and that we do not contradict it in practice.

The Result of this Revelation

God does not reveal the mystery of Christ simply for sermon material or theological treaties or doctrinal outlines. Nor does He even reveal it as a kind of ideal, a theory which is good to keep in one's mind but which is impossible to realise down here on this earth. God reveals the mystery of Christ for the obedience of faith. That is what we read in that Roman letter in chapter 16:25, 26. Paul closes this tremendous letter with those wonderful words which the Holy Spirit so gloriously inspired. He ends like this: "... according to my gospel and the preaching of Jesus Christ, according to the revelation of the mystery which hath been kept in silence through times eternal, but now is manifested ... unto obedience of faith." So the response that God looks for in our hearts is not a mental assent. It is the obedience of faith. This challenge is not only inescapable, but it demands a response. That response is the obedience of faith. I do not think anybody would ever be able to truly respond to the revelation of the mystery of Christ apart from the obedience of faith. There has to be faith.

When God said to Abraham, "Get thee out," in one sense Abraham did not see the mystery of Christ, but there was something which he did see. He saw the city which has the foundations, which has something to do with this mystery of Christ. If God had not created divine faith in his heart, there could have been no obedience, but by faith he obeyed to go out, not knowing whither he went. It has to be the same with you and with me. The heart of this whole matter is that having been saved by the grace of God and made one with the Lord Jesus Christ, we need to grow to full stature. Did you get that? That is the heart of this whole matter.

You see, the mystery of Christ is simply this: we have been made fellow-members of the body. We have been brought into a position where we are partakers of the divine nature, as the apostle Peter says in II Peter 1:4. It is a tremendous and glorious privilege that has been given to us by the grace of God. You and I have been made one with the Lord Jesus, heirs of God, joint heirs with Christ. We have been made fellow-members of the body. We have been brought into Him and, as it were, we have been made His body. Think of that! There is no meaning for a body without the head. In one sense, even when we look at the Lord Jesus as head, there is no meaning to a head without a body. The point of the body is that it has a head and the point of the head is that it is joined to a body. So there is this marvellous union into which you and I have been brought. It is to be, on the one side, like being the bride of Christ. We are to come into such an intimate union with Him, such a direct union with Him, such a communion with Him that it is just like a marriage in which we are given His name. We are joined to Him. We become one with Him—the two become one. The apostle Paul alludes to this when he says (Ephesians 5:31–32):

> ... a man leave his father and mother, and shall cleave to his wife; and the two shall become one flesh. This mystery is great: but I speak in regard of Christ and of the church.

That is one side of this glorious mystery, but the other side is that we are to become the city of God. This bride that we read of in Revelation 21 or 22 is the New Jerusalem, the holy city. It is the city of God. A city is something quite different to a bride. It has an altogether different symbolism. A city is the centre of administration. It is the heart of national intercourse. It is the commercial centre of a nation, as well as the administrative centre of a nation. So, we come into something just as wonderful. Not only has the Lord saved us to bring us into a union with Himself so intimate that it can only be described as a marriage, but He wants to bring us into such a position in Himself that we become His eternal government so that with His Son we reign from the throne.

It is not the kind of picture you often get of people all sitting on thrones, draped in finery and sort of exhibiting themselves before everybody. That is not the idea you get in Scripture. That is the world's idea of kingship. The biblical idea of kingship is service, so we have this amazing picture of eternal service, of divine service, a city at the heart of a re-created universe, a new heaven and a new earth wherein dwells righteousness. At the heart of it is an administration, a government, a throne, and those who have been trained for that government and qualified for that government. Now, I don't know whether you have ever noticed these little words but you see that it is true.

What is the Challenge?

If this is true, then what is the challenge? Now consider this very carefully. This may make all the difference between you really getting a kind of bomb that starts you moving on with God for the rest of your spiritual life, or of you just sitting in a kind of static way for the rest of your life. This mystery is not revealed to tickle our brains. It is not revealed that we might have a sort of blowout in the mind: Boom! That was terrific! However, many people think, "Mystery? Why, what is he spending all this time talking about the mystery of Christ for? That is all theoretical. That is all mystical, that is all *up there!*" Some people who have got a bent that way, love it like that. "Oh," they say, "it's all up there. Wonderful!" It is a form of escapism from a nation that is ridden with strikes and selfishness, and they are thinking, "Oh, it is all sort-of ... up there." It is a kind of Christian transcendental meditation. It calms our nerves and helps us to escape from the routine, but this is not why this mystery is revealed to you. This mystery is revealed to you because it is concrete reality. It is more real than your little humdrum routine life here. It is absolute reality into which you have been brought by the grace of God.

If this is true, then you need to be trained. You cannot put people into governmental positions or administrative positions who have not been educated. You have got to be educated. You have got to be trained. You have got to be qualified. You have got to grow. You have got to come to what this book calls *maturity*, or the old word used in the Authorized Version, *perfection*. Just take your Bible, your New Testament and just look at a few of these scriptures and see if, in fact, in the word of God you do not find some of these things. For instance, in Ephesians 4:13:

... till we all attain unto the unity of the faith, and of the

knowledge of the Son of God, unto a fullgrown man, unto
the measure of the stature of the fulness of Christ ...

Look again, in Colossians 1:27–28:

... to whom God was pleased to make known what is the
riches of the glory of this mystery among the Gentiles, which
is Christ in you, the hope of glory: whom we proclaim,
admonishing every man and teaching every man in all
wisdom, that we may present every man perfect in Christ ...

That we may present every man perfect in Christ. This mystery is not just something static. It is something into which we are brought which we have to come to maturity in Him.

Now if that is so, then I suggest that there is a great deal of which you and I need to take note. It is the same thought again in Philippians 3:12–14. This is one of the most remarkable passages of the New Testament because here, the apostle Paul opens his heart and gives his testimony. There are very few places (except in the book of Acts) where you have the testimony of the apostle Paul. Nowhere is it more fully given than here—the spiritual character of this man. Listen to him:

Not that I have already obtained, or am already made
perfect: but I press on, if so be that I may lay hold on that
for which also I was laid hold on by Christ Jesus. Brethren,
I count not myself yet to have laid hold: but one thing [I do],
forgetting the things which are behind, and stretching forward

to the things which are before, I press on toward the goal
unto the prize of the high calling of God in Christ Jesus.

What is he talking about? Earlier on in this testimony he says, "I count this and this and this and this but refuse that I may win Christ." (see verses 7–8). But then we say to ourselves: but you do not win Christ. Christ is the unspeakable gift of God given to us by the grace of God. We do not win Him. We do not have to do things to win Christ, do we? We are saved by the grace of God when we ask for forgiveness, when we bow before Him in confession and repentance. So, what is he talking about, "that I may win Christ?" Then he speaks about, "... that I may attain unto the resurrection from among the dead?" Literally, it is the "out-resurrection from among the dead." What on earth is he talking about? We are all going to be raised from the dead. So, what is he talking about, "... that I may attain unto the resurrection from among the dead?" He does not say, "that I may attain unto the resurrection of the dead," he says, "that I may attain unto the resurrection *from among the dead.*" Then he says, "Christ Jesus laid hold on me for something. This was not my salvation. Having saved me, He put His hand upon me because He wanted to do something with me. Now I lay hold on that for which He laid hold on me. I press on." To what? To the goal. Ah, the goal ... now we have got it. So, we are saved by the grace of God, but having been saved, there is now a goal. Reaching the goal is all through the grace of God, but you and I must appropriate every bit of the provision of God if we are going to come to the goal. I press on toward the goal and to the prize of the on-high calling of God in Christ Jesus.

That I May Win Christ

I know that may be a lot for some of you, especially those of you who are young in the Lord, but if you only have your eyes open just a little to a wider horizon, it will change your life. This idea that you and I have just been saved to sort-of sing hymns, say prayers, read the scriptures and if we are very good, witness, then after that there is no more. We die and go to heaven and join an eternal hallelujah chorus forever and ever and ever and ever—just sitting on clouds, playing harps and singing. Now, I do not know about you, but I cannot believe that God created us intelligent human beings to only sing forever. I mean, we love singing, we love to praise the Lord, but God has not created us just simply and only to sing eternally. God made us in His image with a creative genius. We do not even know what the mind of God is for the future, but this we do know: it has something to do with being in His Son and with His Son being in us. It has something to do with being one with Him.

I understand this testimony of the apostle Paul in this way: when he says "... that I may win Christ," he did not mean winning Christ as *Saviour*, he meant that he may win Christ as *Bridegroom*. After having been saved by the grace of God, the apostle Paul may, even after having preached to others, himself be a reject—not a reject from salvation, but a reject from the goal. Now, if we really begin to understand this, it changes our whole mind.

Is the Lord Jesus bringing many sons to glory? Are we to be conformed to the same image from glory to glory? It cannot be without deep and costly experience. I do not know a single human being who has become Christ-like in a kind of fairy-tale, wand-waving operation. You and I, having been saved by the grace of God and how ever many experiences we have of the Holy Spirit, nevertheless, have got to have deep and sometimes bitter experiences by which we are conformed to the image of His Son. But when we go on, it is from glory to glory. Something happens in us and it is not only personal, it is corporate. Such experience is not possible without revelation and practical obedience to the light God gives us. In other words, unless God reveals this matter to us, we are in the dark. But once God reveals this matter to us, then there must be obedience. When there is obedience, then we move on with Him.

Now, you may not understand all that I have said thus far. You may have understood very little of it, but one thing you can get hold of is this: if you trust Him and obey Him, you will get there. It is as simple as that. There are those that can have great understanding of biblical truths but get nowhere. Then there can be those who have very little understanding, but because they learn this one lesson, to trust and obey, like the old Aesop's fable about the hare and the tortoise—the tortoise gets there first—so this matter is important.

To be part of the wife of the Lamb, to be part of the city of God, requires not only that we be born of God, but that we grow to maturity. This requires experience. It requires training. It requires education. We cannot come to the throne without such qualifications. Babes cannot reign, practically. The kingdom of God is filled with little spiritual babes. All they are interested in is spiritual toys, something that they can just hold and look at and be happy with. We have got to grow. There is a time for babyhood.

There is time for the kindergarten, and there is a time for primary school, but after that we have to grow up.

That is what I find so very interesting when you start to look at scriptures like these in Revelation chapter 3, speaking to a born-again church which had grown very lukewarm. The Lord said, "I counsel thee to buy of Me gold refined in the fire" (verse 18). Now why did the Lord say, "I counsel thee to *buy* of Me gold refined in the fire"? Since gold speaks to the divine nature of God, surely it is given to us by the grace of God through the saving work of the Lord Jesus. Yes, but you see, the price is experience. If you look at the end of that book you will find that the city of God is made out of pure gold. So how do you get this gold? You get it through the finished work of the Lord Jesus on the cross, but it is at the price of experience. No other way.

Listen again to what He says in verse 21 of the same chapter, "He that overcometh, I will give to him to sit down with Me in my throne, as I also overcame, and sat down with my Father in His throne." There is an overcoming then, and we have to overcome in the same way that He overcame. If we overcome, we sit down with Him in His throne, as He overcame and sat down in His Father's throne.

When you begin to look at some of these things, you find them everywhere. Revelation 3:12:

He that overcometh, I will make him a pillar in the temple of my God, and he shall go out thence no more: and I will write upon him the name of my God, and the name of the city of my God, the new Jerusalem, which cometh down out of heaven from my God, and mine own new name.

Now, I find that interesting and I cannot help feeling that many Protestants have very sadly overlooked a whole area of teaching which has been the province of the Catholics, and this is one of them. We have put such an accent on grace, that we have produced a whole mentality, a lazy mentality. We are saved by grace; we do not have to do anything. We are saved ... fully fledged. There is no need to go on. We just stay where we are. We have got it all. But does the Book say that? Overcoming surely means some kind of discovery of the grace of God in deeper and deeper and deeper ways. Surely it means that we have to discover the power of the Holy Spirit in deeper and deeper and fuller ways. What does it mean that we must "buy gold" unless we come into experiences where we find our own bankruptcy and have to look to God at the cost of deep experience? Only then will we find that something more of the nature of the Lamb has come into us.

Look again, at another passage in the Word of God in 1 Corinthians 3:11–15:

> *For other foundation can no man lay than that which is laid, which is Jesus Christ. But if any man buildeth on the foundation gold, silver, costly stones, wood, hay, stubble; each man's work shall be made manifest: for the day shall declare it, because it is revealed in fire; and the fire itself shall prove each man's work of what sort it is. If any man's work shall abide which he built thereon, he shall receive a reward. If any man's work shall be burned, he shall suffer loss: but he himself shall be saved; yet so as through fire.*

Now, will you please note that the Lord is not here talking about salvation. He is not even talking about your own personal character. He is talking about what you are putting into the house of God, what you are putting into the body of Christ, and what kind of material you are producing and using in the building. It is all to do with an end. If a man's work, built on the foundation of the Lord Jesus Christ abides, he shall receive a reward. Otherwise, he will be saved—but so as by fire. He comes through with nothing but his salvation. He has lost the goal that the apostle Paul made so much of.

If all this is really so, I begin again to understand Revelation 21:7:

> *He that overcometh shall inherit these things; and*
> *I will be his God, and he shall be my son.*

The Father there does not say, "he shall be My child," He says, "he shall be My son." In other words, those who are babes have grown to the place where they are sons in the administration of God. They have overcome. They have inherited.

You have got the same again, in Revelation 21:18, where it says, "And the building of the wall thereof was jasper: and the city was pure gold, like unto pure glass. The foundations of the wall of the city were adorned with all manner of precious stones." Verse 21: "And the twelve gates were twelve pearls ... and the street of the city was pure gold, as it were, transparent as glass."

Now, this matter of the mystery of Christ is intensely practical. Our whole life: our home life, our work life, our business life, and above all our relationship with one another in the Lord

Jesus, becomes the sphere of our education. The office you are in is no accident. The college you are in is no accident. It is the sphere in which God is educating you. Your home life is not some little appendage, something that somehow is not in the centre of everything, but somehow outside–you come out of it to the church, that is the heart of everything, and you go back to your home, which is somehow not in the flow of everything. It is not so. As I think we shall see in future chapters, every one of these matters is put right into the heart of this matter.

The apostle Paul goes to tremendous lengths to talk about husbands and wives. It has all to do with this mystery. It sounds strange to us. He speaks of wives subjecting themselves to their husbands as the church does to Christ and husbands loving their wives as Christ loved the church. They have to care for their wives as their own body, just as Christ cares for the church. He even goes on to fathers and their children, and children and their parents. Then he goes on to the workaday relationships, which would have been much more difficult for us in those days than they are today, even with all our problems, because in those days it was a slave/owner relationship. He speaks of masters and slaves and the kind of relationship they had. It is not as if he is saying, "All of this is right." What he is saying is that this is the sphere in which God works the most precious works in His children and brings them to a place where they are trained, disciplined, and qualified. It is where, through deep experience, they come to the place where they can reign with Christ. Now, it is down here that all this has to happen and if it does not happen down here, there is no hope for us.

Practical Relevance of the Mystery

The practical relevance of all this is really tremendous. It is an amazing thing that this mystery of Christ is far from being some mystical, abstract, vague, ethereal thing somewhere up there. It is a matter of knowing Christ and knowing one another in Christ in the area in which we live. Many people become spiritual butterflies. They flip from company [church assembly] to company, sucking the spiritual nectar here and there, or sometimes being bored stiff. But they escape all responsibility and all discipline. It is a very nice thing to be able to go from place to place and to be able just to judge what is going on. They say, "I didn't think much of that." Or, "Don't you think that was tremendous?" When there is a bit of blessing, "Oh," we say, "it was wonderful. We were there when that tremendous moving of the Spirit of God came amongst those people. We were there." However, it does not mean anything to heaven because it was never worked out in relationship with one another.

This matter of the local expression of this is just tremendous. It has to be expressed locally. It is the easiest thing in the world to say that you would love the saints in Hong Kong. Anyone can love the saints in Hong Kong, they are thousands of miles away. You can love the saints in Newcastle because they happen to be a few hundred miles away. God says, "It does not mean anything to Me. It is whether you can love the saints where you are living." If you cannot, I will tell you a secret ... you will never love those in Newcastle either, once you live with them. That is where we are all found out in this thing. Some people find it easier to put a little bit of money towards some missionary effort on the other side of the world but they would not dream of calling on a neighbour and helping them. They would not dream of witnessing for the Lord. It is much easier to pay for something else miles away, but it is this local expression that is so tremendously important.

This matter of where we live is very important. It is one of the things God showed us right at the beginning when we began to gather together—the local nature of the expression of the church. When we start to travel in from great distances, we can all do this in times when there is no emergency, and no civil strife, or no war; of course, we can drive here. People say, "Well, does it matter? We have got a car; we can get in very easily. It does not seem to matter. We will be alright; we can get in swiftly." Compromise comes in. Then comes trouble—no petrol—and when you have got children, you have an added problem. How do you get in?

Now if I read my Bible aright, I understand that we are moving more and more into those days when we are going to have civil emergencies, when there is going to be strife, and when there is going to be war. Therefore, this whole matter of living in close proximity is essential. If we feel that God has called us to this part of the family, then we have to be very practical about it. Now, I know people will say, "Well, that is very easy for him to say that. Does he know what it costs? It is much easier to have a place right out on the fringe of things." But this is where we are forced by circumstances to compromise and, in the end, we are always found out by compromise.

The Scripture says there will be earthquakes. Well, thank God, we do not live in an earthquake region. That is very selfish, but I mean, we sort of say, "Well, Britain's not in an earthquake region." (Where I live for part of the year is right on one of the major faults.

Of course, anytime it could happen but for the grace of God.) But here there is no earthquake. Okay, but it says there will be earthquakes in diverse places. It says there will be wars. It says there will be famines. We sometimes think of famines as only famines of food, but maybe it will be a famine of energy. Now, if that kind of thing comes, suddenly we realise the value of being near to one another.

Do you begin to realise what we are saying? These truths that God has revealed to us about the mystery of Christ in its practical outworking are not things on which we can compromise. We do so at our own peril. We can get away with it because there is a shortcut, but in the long term, we will suffer. It is a tremendous thing in times of war, if you are an older sister on your own, to be near to others who can just walk around to you and see that you are alright. What are we going to do if people are miles away? We cannot walk there. The telephones may be destroyed. You may not be able to communicate. People do not think of these things. Here is a mother with two or three children far away somewhere. How is anyone going to get there? "Well, you see, we will phone through to some local company and get them to go around!" You won't be able to do it. There are many of these practical things.

This mystery of Christ may all sound very wonderful and you might say, "Oh, it's glorious. We are one with the Lord Jesus, we are united to Him. We have been made partakers of the divine nature and we are one body in Christ. Isn't it marvellous?" But then it comes down to the actual practical side of it: our unity. That is the heart of the whole thing—our real unity. There are no sex barriers, no national barriers, no racial barriers, no colour barriers, no social barriers, no age barriers—one Christ. Now we shall have some problems when you look at it like that. We begin to say, "Now, we have some problems; we are living in the 20th century." Exactly, but you see, we have to discover how this works out, what are the ways in which it works out?

For instance, take this question of government. The mystery of Christ is a matter of government. It is a matter of being under the Headship of Jesus. It speaks of growing up into Him as head, from whom the whole body ... or holding fast the head. But you know, we are living in a day where authority is no longer respected or obeyed, in days of growing anarchy. This spirit comes right into the house of God as well. Now you know as well as I do, that I do not believe in this heavy-handed authority, this pyramid structure that some believe in, where everyone is submitted to somebody and where, really, in the end, you end up with a kind of police state. But you can go the other way too. In the house of God, there is order. How can anyone occupy a position of authority in the ages to come in a new heaven and a new earth if they have not learned to be under authority down here? Do you think that God will put under you a whole number of people and say, "Now, you are responsible for those thousands of people, or hundreds of people, or perhaps millions of people," when you yourself have never been under another person's authority?

We learn our greatest lessons when we need to recognise the Headship of Jesus as it is found in our brothers and sisters. It is the hardest lesson of all because we are all so frail and so weak. We do not have to look very far to find all the flaws and all the weaknesses and all the failings which excuse us from having to obey or submit in any way. Now you understand what I am trying to say. All this is the practical relevance of the mystery of Christ. If we are members of the body, then each part has to function. If you have never functioned down here and never, never been a joint of supply, never given anything, never passed on anything, never shared anything, how can you be in this body of the Lord, this bride of Christ, this wife of the Lamb, this city of God? What are we going to do in eternity?

Well, you begin to see that there are some quite practical questions raised by all this. I sometimes think that we folks believe that by just attending a meeting, just listening to a Bible study, putting in an appearance at the prayer meeting, we are actually involved in this matter. Thank God that everyone who is born again is potentially in the bride of Christ, but we have to go places. We have to go places, not only personally, but corporately. It is in our relationship with one another that this is all finally brought to its acid test. We do not have very many years left to us, to allow God to do the kind of work that needs to be done in our lives. I do not know if you feel like I do, but I think back on many, many wasted opportunities—time that has been frittered away and wasted. God alone can wake us up on this, and by His grace bring us face-to-face with the real issues. May the Lord help you, and may He help me also in this matter. Shall we pray?

Lord, we do pray that Thou wilt really bring the challenge of this whole matter home to us. Lord, we pray that in some way, Thou wilt create in our hearts that obedience of faith. Lord, Thou knowest how it is very easy for us, somehow or other, to fritter away our lives, even when we are saved, playing about with divine things, just on the circumference, always dithering, never really coming into what

Thou hast for us. Lord, deliver us we pray! Oh, by Thy Holy Spirit, so move in our hearts, so fall upon us, that we shall, Lord, be enabled to wake up and face the challenge and to face it with the obedience of faith. Lord, help us in this matter, we pray. We commit this to Thee, oh Lord, and we pray that it may not be wasted or misspent in any way. Forgive weakness, Lord, and grant that Thy Word might get right into our hearts in such a way that there will be a consequence and a result that will be eternal. We ask all this in the name of our Lord Jesus. Amen.

4.
The Oneness
of Christ in Action

Ephesians 3:1–11:

For this cause I Paul, the prisoner of Christ Jesus in behalf of you Gentiles,—if so be that ye have heard of the dispensation of that grace of God which was given me to you-ward; how that by revelation was made known unto me the mystery, as I wrote before in few words, whereby, when ye read, ye can perceive my understanding in the mystery of Christ; which in other generations was not made known unto the sons of men, as it hath now been revealed unto his holy apostles and prophets in the Spirit; [to wit], that the Gentiles are fellow-heirs, and fellow-members of the body, and fellow-partakers of the promise in Christ Jesus through the gospel, whereof I was made a minister, according to the gift of that grace of God which was given me according to the working of his power. Unto me, who am less than the least of all saints, was this grace given, to preach unto the Gentiles the unsearchable riches of Christ; and to make all men see what is

*the dispensation of the mystery
which for ages hath been hid
in God who created all things;
to the intent that now unto the
principalities and the powers in
the heavenly [places] might be
made known through the church
the manifold wisdom of God,
according to the eternal purpose
which he purposed in Christ
Jesus our Lord.*

Colossians 1:24–2:3

*Now I rejoice in my sufferings
for your sake, and fill up on my
part that which is lacking of
the afflictions of Christ in my
flesh for his body's sake, which
is the church; whereof I was
made a minister, according to
the dispensation of God which
was given me to you-ward, to
fulfil the word of God, [even]
the mystery which hath been hid
for ages and generations: but
now hath it been manifested to
his saints, to whom God was
pleased to make known what
is the riches of the glory of this
mystery among the Gentiles,
which is Christ in you, the hope
of glory: whom we proclaim,
admonishing every man and
teaching every man in all
wisdom, that we may present
every man perfect in Christ;
whereunto I labor also, striving
according to his working, which
worketh in me mightily. For
I would have you know how
greatly I strive for you, and for
them at Laodicea, and for as
many as have not seen my face
in the flesh; that their hearts
may be comforted, they being
knit together in love, and unto
all riches of the full assurance
of understanding, that they
may know the mystery of God,
[even] Christ, in whom are all
the treasures of wisdom and
knowledge hidden.*

Now shall we just bow our heads in prayer this evening as we, in our own hearts, all look to the Lord that He will be with us this night in this study, and give revelation and illumination? Let us just bow our heads to be definite with the Lord. If you are specific with the Lord, the Lord will be specific with you.

Dear Lord, we do want to thank Thee that when we come to Thy Word we have a sure and certain promise that, Lord, Thou wilt, by the Spirit of Truth, lead us into all truth. We want to tell Thee Lord that apart from the gracious ministry of the Holy Spirit neither our speaking nor our hearing, will be to any profit. But, oh Father, how glad we are that when the Holy Spirit is here, with enabling power and grace, then our speaking can be the speaking of Thy Word. It can be an opening of a door of utterance to speak the mystery of Christ and it can be, to us who hear, revelation and illumination so that, Lord, our hearts, the eyes of our hearts are enlightened and we know Thyself in a way that we have never known before. So, Lord we commit this little time to Thee that Thou wilt, Lord, dispel any darkness, heaviness, of any kind, and Thou wilt grant instead that we may meet with Thee. We ask it in Jesus' name, amen.

This matter of the mystery of Christ, although it spans the whole of time from before times eternal and right through to the ages to come, is not a mystical matter. In other words, because we call it the "mystery of Christ," people immediately think that it is a mystical matter, something which only those who are a bit barmy [slightly crazy] can understand. You have to have your head in the clouds like one of those dreamy, visionary type of people who are of no earthly use. They think that if you are that type of person—

poetic or artistic—then you will be the kind of person that will understand the mystery of Christ. (I am not saying that is true.) If you are practical, down to earth, dealing in concrete terms, the sort of practical "Martha" type, then of course this mystery of Christ is not for you. You will never understand it and you might as well have a little sleep instead of seeking to understand this mystery. No, this is not so.

The mystery of Christ is not a secret which God withholds from people. It is not something which is mystical in the sense that it is abstract, ethereal, somehow "up there" somewhere. It is a secret which God has communicated and wants to communicate to every born-again believer in this age. What has been hidden from other ages and other generations, God has now revealed through His holy apostles and prophets. This is the most wonderful privilege that every true child of God has in this age. That which was withheld from Abraham, Isaac, Jacob, Moses, and from the other great patriarchs and prophets, even John the Baptist, has been revealed to the humblest, simplest, and most insignificant child of God. Is that not marvellous? No wonder the Lord Jesus said that the least in the kingdom of God is greater than John the Baptist. He did not mean that you and I are of more spiritual value than Abraham or Isaac or Jacob. He did not mean that we have more spiritual character than Isaiah or Zechariah or John the Baptist himself. What the Lord meant was that the simplest, most insignificant child of God in the kingdom has more privilege than all those patriarchs and prophets put together because it has been our tremendous privilege to have this mystery communicated to us.

Now, it is a tragedy when the children of God do not even know what it is all about. This matter lies at the heart of the gospel. It lies at the heart of God's purpose. It lies at the heart of His redeeming grace. Therefore, since it is a privilege that God has revealed to us, every one of us, as soon as we are saved, should begin to seek the Lord for illumination, should begin to seek the Lord for revelation. We should seek the Lord that this secret, which He has so graciously manifested, revealed and communicated, might be known to me and might be known to you.

This mystery is not something vague or idealistic, something theoretical. Yet, this is how most people think of the mystery of Christ. They think, "Oh, it is a wonderful, wonderful, spiritual ideal, a wonderful truth, but basically theoretical." Those that would go further than that would say, "It is a wonderful truth, but it is something to do with the future after death. It is not anything that you and I can enter into now." But that is not true. The mystery of Christ, if I understand it aright, is intensely practical, and it has a very real relevance to us all now. So, without any further introduction, I want to start to consider some of its relevance in practice for us.

The first thing I want to mention is that the mystery of Christ is the oneness of Christ in action. Let me say it again: the mystery of Christ is the oneness of Christ in action. The mystery of godliness, the mystery of Christ is that by the grace of God, you and I have been brought into a union with Him. There should be fruit from that union. There should be love, joy, peace, long-suffering, which is the fruit of the Spirit that comes out of that union. Because we are one with Christ—I am one with Christ, you are one with Christ—then something has happened between us. If I and the

Lord Jesus have become one and you and the Lord Jesus have become one, then something has happened to you and me. We have become one and there should be fruit from that.

Now you begin to understand why the enemy attacks this matter. I do not suppose there is any matter that is more furiously, ferociously attacked than the unity of God's people. I travel all over the place, and it is rare to find the Lord's people staying together. In moments of great blessing, people do come together and they stay together for a while, but not for long. It is not so very long before they fall out with one another, when they begin to come down to the basics. So often in Christian circles, we sneer at the United Nations. We say, "United Nations, no ... dis-united nations." But in actual fact, we are no better. We believers are just as hopelessly divided at times.

This mystery of Christ is nothing if it is not the oneness of the Lord Jesus in action. Essentially, the mystery of Christ is union with Christ. We have become one body in Christ as it says in Romans 12:5: "... although we have many members, yet are we one body in Christ." Not one body *of* Christ, one body *in* Christ. That is something more. We have it again in 1 Corinthians 12:12:

For as the body is one, and hath many
members, and all the members of the body, being
many, are one body; so also is Christ.

Is that not amazing? It did not say, "so also is the body of Christ." He did not say, "so also is the body of which Christ is the head." What that says is this: the body *is* Christ. Because we are in Him, therefore, He *is* our oneness, He *is* our life, He *is* our salvation.

In some marvellous way we have been incorporated, we have been made the body of the Lord Jesus. We have come into Him; we have become partakers of Him. We have become members of Him, and therefore members of one another; we have become limbs of the Lord Jesus. It is amazing. One hardly dares to say this if it were not the Word of God. We are limbs one of another. I say that is tremendous. Now, that is what the Word of God says.

The Nature of Oneness

The nature of this oneness is tremendous. It is not a goal to be attained, or a state to be achieved. So very often amongst the Lord's people you hear about the unity of the people of God as a goal that we are all trying to reach. We have organisations, ecumenical organisations, and many other agencies that are seeking to promote this unity. They are seeking somehow or other to move us phase by phase, stage by stage into some kind of unity. But this oneness of Christ is not a goal, an ideal that we are all seeking to realise, a kind of goal which we are seeking to attain, a state that we are seeking to achieve. This oneness is something into which we are born of God by the Spirit.

Now when we understand that truth, our whole mentality changes. You see, it is not an outward organisational unity, something that exists because we have a worldwide structure with a worldwide headquarters, with a worldwide uniformity. No! This oneness, this unity is an organic, living, vital unity into which we are introduced by a new birth. So, the simplest child of God is in this unity. It is not something to be achieved, but something to be maintained. No wonder the apostle said, "give diligence to maintain the unity of the Spirit." He did not say, "Now then, all of you muster up every bit of faith that you have, take hold of all the grace that is yours, and try to create the unity of the Spirit. Try to achieve the unity of the Spirit." No, what he said was, "Give diligence to keep the unity of the Spirit." You cannot keep something you have not already got. Or in the modern version it also says, "Maintain the unity of the Spirit." You cannot maintain something you do not have already. The very word presupposes that it is already there. Is this not wonderful?

Now you begin to look at a few scriptures, and they begin to fall into place. Consider John 17 and these wonderful words of our Lord's high priestly prayer that are so tremendous. He prays "... for them also that believe on Me through their word," (that is you and me) "that they may all be one" (see verses 20, 21a). Now He goes on, "... even as thou, Father, art in me, and I in thee, that they also may be in us" (see verse 21b). He continues, "... that the world may believe that thou didst send me. And the glory which thou hast given me I have given unto them; that they may be one, even as we are one; I in them, and thou in me, that they may be perfected into one; that the world may know that thou didst send me, and lovedst them, even as thou lovedst me" (see verses 21–23).

Now, I think that is an amazing statement of our Lord because the Lord Jesus was saying that it is something that no theological mind has ever yet been able to fathom or plumb. What our Lord was saying is as simple as this: the unity that exists between the Father and the Son is the unity into which you and I are born by the Spirit of God. You cannot organise that. You cannot attain to that. Only the grace of God could do that. Only the finished work of the Lord Jesus could introduce you into something like that. If you were the dearest, sweetest patriarch in the world, someone who gave his or her whole life to God, you still would not achieve a goal like that! To be introduced into the same unity that exists between the Father and the Son? No! A church creed has not yet been able to define the unity of the Godhead. We only know that there is one God, but three persons. We do not understand it. They have tried to define it this way and have tried to define it another way. I am not pouring any scorn upon their definitions because I believe the Holy Spirit has helped them, but even when you read their definitions it leaves you bewildered. But the Lord Jesus said, "I pray for them." This is the prayer of the Lord Jesus; this is the burden of His intercession. What does He pray? "That they may be one, even as Thou Father art in Me, and I in Thee, that they may be in us." There, this is the mystery of Christ. No one else ever revealed that. That has been revealed to us. That is tremendous!

If only the Holy Spirit would shine into your heart, the whole matter of the church would suddenly fall into place. You would not see it as a structure, as a place where you can leave your umbrella or your handbag. You would not think that you *go* to church. You would not see it like that anymore. You would suddenly know that the church *is* the Lord Jesus. I mean—I am *in* Him. He is *in* me. We are in Him; He is in us. Then you would begin to realise that it is not a question of labelling it. It is neither Anglican, nor Methodist, nor Lutheran, nor Mennonite, nor anything else. How dare we give it any human name? It is impossible to name it, to devalue what God has done, to make it less than it is in the eyes of God. Oh, if we had only all seen this. Would it not be wonderful? We would have been saved from many pitfalls in church history and many tragic divisions.

Let us come back to this matter again. Turn again to John 15:5. Consider the words of our Lord Jesus again. It was literally in the same hour or two in which He prayed that prayer. Just before it He said this, "I am the vine, ye are the branches." Then He said, "He that abideth in Me and I in him, the same beareth much fruit for apart from me you can do nothing." I know some of you have heard me say this many times, but let me say it again. You see, people read this quite wrongly; they read, "I am the trunk; you are the branches." The Lord never said, "I am the trunk; you are the branches." The Lord said, "I am the vine. You are the branches." The vine is the roots, the trunk, the branches, the tendrils, the leaves, the blossom, and the fruit. It is the totality! Jesus was saying, "I am the whole thing, from root to fruit. I am the whole—Alpha and Omega, beginning and end, first and last. I am it all." Blessed be God, He says, "You are branches. You are not the vine. You are branches. You are much less than Me. But you are in Me." The Lord did not say, "I am the root. I am the trunk. I am the leaves. I am the tendril. I am the blossom and the fruit and you are the branches." He said, "I am the vine." What He was really saying is this, "I am the branches. You are the branches, only I am much more than you." You know Jesus said, "I am the light of the world." He also said, "You are the light of the world." How can we be the light of the world? We understand how He can be the light of the world. How can we be the light of the world? We can only be the light of the world insofar as we are one with Him. When we are in Him and He is in us, we become the light of the world because He is the light of the world, and in us He becomes the light of the world. Do you understand it?

Now, you see this matter of the church is something so wonderful when we begin to see that He is the vine. He is the covenant people of God. In those days, any Jew would have understood when Jesus said, "I am the true vine, my Father is the husbandman." They would have reeled back, as it were, in their mind. Why? Because they knew very well that the vine was the symbol of the covenant people of God. In the only times in Jewish history when Jewish coins were struck, vines were put on them. Every Jew knew: "That speaks of us; that is the symbol of us! We are the covenant people of God."

Then the Lord Jesus came and said, "I am the bread of life" (John 6:35a, 48). Well, alright, we do not quite understand it Lord, but You say that You are the manna that comes down out of heaven, and whoever eats of Your flesh will have eternal life (see verse 51). Well, it is hard to understand, but alright. Then He said, "I am the resurrection and the life" (John 11:25). We say, "Oh, dear!" He did not say, "I give the resurrection, and I give the life, but I am the resurrection and the life." That is rather hard. Then He said, "I am the way the truth and the life" (John 14:6). Well, that is a little difficult. He did not say, "I point to the way, I preach the truth and I give the life." He said, "I am." Then He said, "Before Abraham was I Am." Now, how do we understand it all?

However, I think the thing which must have been the most confusing of all was when He said, "I am the true vine and My Father is the husbandman." It was as if they had said, "Now, we don't understand what He is talking about. The rest was hard enough. But now it has gone to another dimension of difficulty. How can He be the people? How can He *be* the covenant people? But He is saying, 'I am the covenant people and My Father is the husbandman, who from the beginning has cared for this people, watched over this people, attended to this people, sought to prune back what was alive and cut out what is dead.'"

The Lord Jesus was saying the same thing again. This is a unity into which we are born. He did not say, "All who fight to get into Me, I will come into them. If you go on long enough, striving and straining, in the end, you will get into Me and then I'll get into you." He did not say that. He said, "Abide in Me." The word is "remain in Me." You cannot remain somewhere if you are not already there. God has put us there. Now we must remain there. God has positioned us in Christ, now we must abide. We are to stay where God has put us. God has put us in His Christ, and has put His Christ in us.

Now look again at another scripture in 1 Corinthians 12:12–14:

> For as the body is one, and hath many members, and
> all the members of the body, being many, are one
> body; so also is Christ. For in one Spirit were we
> all baptized into one body, whether Jews or Greeks,
> whether bond or free; and were all made to drink of one
> Spirit. For the body is not one member, but many.

Now what is he saying? He is saying that although it is one body, there are many members. Yet this one body with many members is Christ. By one Spirit, we have all been immersed into the one body, we have all been positioned in the one body and we have all been made to drink of the one Spirit. This is amazing, is it not? So, this is the mystery of Christ. The apostle says, "So you can see in a few words, my understanding of this mystery to which," he says ['which is' we would say in modern English], "that we are fellow-heirs, fellow-members, fellow-partakers."

Look again at Romans 12:4–5. Here we have it again in another letter:

> For even as we have many members in one body, and all the members have not the same office: so we, who are many, are one body in Christ, and severally members one of another.

Now that is an interesting word is it not? "And severally members one of another," which means that we are all members of one another. So this is not only that we are members of the Lord Jesus, not only that we have become one body in Him, but something has happened to us. Now we are coming near to this mystery of Christ. We are fellow-members of the body.

I think now, if you begin to think carefully and prayerfully, you will begin to understand the injunction the apostle Paul gave by the Spirit, "Give diligence to keep the unity of the Spirit" (Ephesians 4:3). You may know absolutely nothing. You may have been born of God one hour ago, but if you were born one hour ago, of God, you are in this oneness. You may have been to a theological seminary and may be able to prepare a sermon for Sunday, be reasonably intelligent, but without much living power, if any. If you have not been born of God, you are not in this oneness. You can have the titles, you can have the clothing, you can have the structure, you can have the position. But if you are not born of

God, you are not in that oneness. You may not have the structure, or the titles, or the status, or the training, but if you are born of God, you are in that oneness. I find this a tremendous privilege.

What Unites Believers?

Now, let us then ask ourselves a question. What is it that unites all believers? Think for a moment. Let us look at it from another angle, to see if we can help ourselves in this matter. What is it that unites all believers? Race? No, if there are any with Jewish background and others of Gentile background, we are divided instantly. It is not race. Are we united by colour? No, we are not united by race nor by colour. Then, are we united by nationality? No, it would be very interesting to see the nationalities where we gather locally at Halford House. There are all kinds of nationalities, so we are not united by that. We are not all good "Britishers," so we are not united in that. What are we then? Are we united by social class? No. We are many different classes. Background? Where we came from? We are not united by that. So, by what are we united? Well, then perhaps we are united by theological views. But if there is someone here who has strong Calvinistic views, and someone else who has strong Arminian views, we are not united. Maybe there is someone here who believes fervently in baptism by sprinkling, and many others who believe that you should be baptised as a believer by immersion. Well, we are not united by that either.

So, what are we going to do? We may be born of God but we are not united by that. There are many other views that I will not go into. Some believe in a millennium and do so very fervently.

Others do not believe in a millennium at all. They think it is nonsense! Well, what are we going to do? Tear each other's eyes out? They do in some places. What shall we do? Some people believe we are going to go before the tribulation, and some people believe we are going to go after the tribulation and some during the tribulation. What shall we do? There are many other matters, theological matters, that are just as difficult. So on those matter we are not one. What about denominational labels? Well, I suppose we have all kinds of denominational labels, some let them go, others still have them.

Oh, what is it then that unites us? Temperament? Now, we know very well, if we are honest, that this is the root of half of our problems! There are people that are so full of zeal and energy, they will go ahead and do something! Then there are others that are so cautious. Of course, those who go forward believe that the people who are cautious just have an evil heart of unbelief; and those who have that kind of inbuilt caution believe that they have got wisdom. But I have seen companies [assemblies of the Lord's people] torn in shreds by temperament, when people cannot recognise temperament under the government of God. Oh, temperament is a big thing. You have some people who are melancholic—down they go—and nothing on earth will drag them up. When we are all praising the Lord, they are enjoying their time down at the bottom of the ocean. But then they will come up and they rise to dizzy heights, where they almost seem to be stupid! Whilst others of us, like tanks, move along on a level course. Not such a wide variation of feeling, neither too much down, nor too much up. It is terribly difficult, when you have got someone who is a true melancholic and someone who is a true phlegmatic, to get them to understand one another. The melancholic feels the phlegmatic is the type of person who could never ever feel anything. The phlegmatic feels that the melancholic is one of those stupid artistic types who are not worth too much. Always up there or down there and rarely on the level. But we are not united by temperament.

So, what are we united by? Well, what about age? We are not united by age, are we? Really, I mean, we have a whole range here and going up nearly to the 90's. What about sex? No, we are not united by that, either. So, what is it that unites us? There is only one Person who unites us—it is Christ. You see, we may be different races, different colours, different nationalities, different social backgrounds, different theological persuasions, different ages, different sexes, but there is only one Lord Jesus. The glory of this matter is that everyone who is born of God is in the same Lord Jesus and the same Lord Jesus is in all of them. So here is a melancholic, he is in the Lord Jesus. Here is a phlegmatic, he is in the same Lord Jesus, and the same Lord Jesus is in the phlegmatic and in the melancholic. So, there is their unity. Their unity is not temperament, nor bashing one another to try and make each other the same as the other. Their unity lies in resting in the fact that they are quite different, but they have the same Lord.

Now, whatever women's lib may say, women are quite different to men. That is their glory. The fact of the matter is this: we can start along that line which the world is going along that we are totally equal. We *are* equal. I firmly believe that, whatever some may teach that we are not equal, we are absolutely equal, because our status before God is absolutely the same. Our worth before

God is absolutely the same, but our function is different. Women complement men and men complement women. They are two halves of a whole. Now, what is the uniting factor which will destroy all the bitterness? It is the Lord Jesus because men are in Christ and women are in Christ; Christ is in the men and He is in the women. Do you understand?

What about age? There are the youngsters that do not feel much relationship to the older ones. They do not feel they can approach them. They somehow feel they belong to another age. Is it not wonderful when we begin to realise that this older person is in the same Lord Jesus as this younger person, whoever it is, is in. Do you understand? The same Lord Jesus is in us all. So suddenly, we begin to realise that everybody has got something to give. The older person has got something to give; the younger person has got something to give. It is not as if the older people have only got something to give and the younger people have nothing to give. The young people, you younger ones, also have a lot to give. You can rejuvenate the older ones who do need it at times. You can rejuvenate them, you can refresh them, you can renew them and they can give you depth that you cannot have with youth; not imposing upon you, not destroying your initiative, or your freedom of action, but giving a security and a balance. But the only way we can stay together is in the Lord Jesus. When young and old see it is the Lord Jesus—this same Lord Jesus—we are in Him together, and He is in us together, then we begin to see the value of one another.

All these wretched things, the spirit of the age, which is destroying society with bitterness, do not have to have any place in the house of God. But the house of God becomes a testimony to the world that young and old can be together, that men and women can find their rightful place together, that different theological persuasions can remain together, that different colours can worship and live together, that different races, different nationalities can all be found together. I sometimes feel like crying when I hear, amongst the Lord's people, this kind of talk about the world and how divided it is, how disunited it is and how it is all going on the broad way that leads to destruction, when we ourselves, who should be a testimony to a dynamic unity, are as divided as the world. Only we have less reason. We have no reason to be divided because our unity is not something we have to achieve or attain. It is something which we were born into. That is why the mystery of Christ is the oneness of Christ in action. It is meant to be a dynamic power in society, because as the world looks on, they see there the kind of society that God meant the world to have, only from which they fell. In the church with all our failings and faults, because we are frail human beings, the world ought to be able to see the kind of unity, the kind of love, the kind of care that attracts them.

Yes, you see, Christ is our basic oneness never forget that. That is why the apostle Paul, when he came to the church in Corinth and found that they were divided in four ways (there was the Peter party, there was the Paul party, there was the Apollos party and there was the exclusive party) (see 1 Corinthians 3:4, 5) he said, "I determined not to know anything among you save Jesus Christ and Him crucified." What was his point? Well, you say, "Can Christ be divided?" No. Therefore, Paul would say, "All those who were born again in Apollos' party, they belong to me and I to them. All in my own party that have taken my name, I belong to them and they to me, and they belong to the others and the others to them. Also, Peter's party, I belong to them, and they to me because I determine not to know anything save Jesus Christ and Him crucified."

You see, as I have often tried to put it in a kind of basic mathematics, it is you, plus another and another and another in Christ, and Christ in you and Christ in another and another, equals the church. That is the church. Now within Christ, all these middle walls of partition, all these middle walls which divide us, have been abolished. For instance, look at Ephesians 2:14–15:

> For he is our peace, who made both one, and brake
> down the middle wall of partition, having abolished
> in his flesh the enmity, even the law of commandments
> contained in ordinances; that he might create in
> himself of the two one new man, so making peace.

The middle of all of partition has gone. There was no greater middle wall of partition than between Jew and Gentile, that was a colossal wall of partition. If that dividing wall is gone, so have all the others. Look again at John 10:16:

> And other sheep I have, which are not of this fold:
> them also I must bring, and they shall hear my voice;
> and they shall become one flock, one shepherd.

Is that not interesting? One flock, one shepherd. Because there is one shepherd, there will be one flock. The middle wall is gone!

The middle wall is gone. The middle wall that divides is gone! Some were outside, some were in; some were inside, some were far off; some were alienated, some were favoured. It is gone. Look again at Colossians 3:10–11:

> *... and have put on the new man, that is being*
> *renewed unto knowledge after the image of him that*
> *created him: where there cannot be Greek and Jew,*
> *circumcision and uncircumcision, barbarian, Scythian,*
> *bondman, freeman; but Christ is all, and in all.*

Now, do you realise the walls between those people? Greek and Jew have a colossal wall between them. There are racial walls, religious walls, circumcision and uncircumcision, total theological and religious differences.

Barbarian, Scythian—oh, my! They were beyond the pale. They were the vandals. They were the uncultured ones. They were just considered to be like savages. Do you mean to tell me that the apostle Paul is saying that this savage, in Christ, has no middle wall dividing him from us? We, with our education, and sophistication, and refinement, and standards of living? Surely, it cannot mean such a thing! But that is what it says.

Could there be any greater difference than between a bondman and a freeman? You know what a freeman was? He was someone who was completely free, but a bondman was owned by his master. He could not go out free. I cannot think of any greater difference in social class than to be a bondslave or to be a free citizen. A free citizen had status, position in the whole community; a bondslave had none. Yet it says the middle wall is gone. Now, does this mean that in those days bondslaves were no longer bondslaves? Oh, no. They were still bondslaves. The apostle Paul goes on into his letters to tell bondslaves how to react to their masters! Some of them were debauched, depraved men and yet he tells them how to look beyond them, through them, to the Master behind and serve the Lord and serve those evil men as if it was the Lord Himself. So, they remained bondmen. You see it says in Galatians 3:27–28:

> For as many of you as were baptized into Christ did
> put on Christ. There can be neither Jew nor Greek, there
> can be neither bond nor free, there can be no male
> and female; for ye all are one man in Christ Jesus.

So, people tell us that of course that means there is no lady. There are no ladies anymore, no men. We are a new man. But it does not say that. I shall believe a woman is a man or a man is a woman when a man can give birth to a child. Then I will join women's lib. But if a man cannot give birth to a child himself, then there must be a difference in function! There must be a difference in constitution, there must be some difference in emotional makeup. So, what does it mean when he says there is neither male or female in Christ? It means that the middle wall of all of bitterness has gone, the middle wall of discrimination has gone, the middle wall of alienation has gone, the division has gone but the functions remain. Those who are Jewish, remain Jewish. Those who are Greeks, remain Greeks, but they are one new man in Christ; the middle wall has gone. You are not meant to give up being British because you are a Christian. You are meant to render unto God what is God's, and unto Caesar what is Caesar's. Where the two things come into conflict, then your priority is God, not Caesar. Nevertheless, you do not lose your British citizenship, or your Norwegian citizenship, or your German citizenship, or your Chinese citizenship, or your American citizenship, your Canadian citizenship, or your Australian citizenship. (I will not go any further.) You do not give it up. You not only retain it, you have a duty and a mandate given you by God to vote and to make yourself, your little voice, known in your country. So much for these people who never listen to the news and never vote because they are the Lord's people. What nonsense! You are to obey every ordinance of man for the Lord's sake.

So, you see, we do not lose these things. What happens? The thing that has divided us and become the fountain of bitterness amongst us is destroyed. It is removed, it is abolished, and we are one in Him. He becomes our oneness. Christ is everything in everyone. Now as Christ is everything in the Jew who is saved and everything in the Gentile who is saved, if Christ is everything in the bondman and everything in the free citizen, and everything in the barbarian, Scythian, and everything in the cultured type, everything in the circumcised and everything in the uncircumcised, what a fullness we have! Oh, I hope that you begin to see something of what this means. Let us just list these things: it means that racial and national differences have been abolished, social differences have been abolished, theological differences have been abolished, the sex barrier has been abolished, the age barrier has been abolished, and temperamental differences have been abolished.

United—with Differences

Now I do not mean that there are not different temperaments, do you understand me? Not at all. What I am simply saying is this: for instance, the person who sometimes is a person who gets depressed, does not always have to feel that they have to be full of froth and bubble! There are times when it is normal and natural to go down. Of course, when a person has an unhealthy love for being down, as some do, there is something wrong. It is an obsession. But generally speaking, we can be ourselves in the Lord, can we not? This brings a tremendous relief to us all. For the first time we can start to just sort of say, "Oh, I can breathe again! I can be myself. I know I've got to be tempered. I've got to be motivated. There's got to be adjustments, the excesses and extremes have got to be ironed out. But what I am, I am!" I remain what I am, and you remain what you are. We come together and then there is fullness in this whole matter!

For instance, I do not think it is too bad a thing at all when we have some who see and emphasise very much on the predestinating power of God. It is one end of the truth. Somewhere on the other end, this whole matter of human responsibility and freewill is also found. Now personally, I do not see that other end so well, but I know there are those, even amongst us here, who see it very clearly, and I think that is right. Why should one person not accentuate and emphasise the sovereignty of God in all things and another person emphasise human responsibility, the necessity of human response? If God has led that person that way and another, another way, what else can you do?

As I have sometimes told you, I remember years ago a man who was the father of famous sons. One son was quite famous, the other a very well-known Navy Captain who was nowhere near God. He came back one day in a drunken state, fell on his living room floor in a stupor, came round the next morning with a hangover—converted. Converted! He could not think what had happened to him, except for the first time he wanted to pray, and then he began to read the Bible. Well, you do not blame him for becoming a Calvinist, do you? What else could he become? He never signed a decision card. He never went forward at a rally; he never responded. He told me the story himself. His wife told me, "But you listen to mine! A few days later, as I was doing the hall, I couldn't think what had happened to Charles. I leant on top of the broom and I thought to myself, 'What has happened to my husband?'" She said, "Suddenly, I was converted." Now, when people tell me, "Oh, no, no, somewhere or other, he must have responded." I do not know. They say the same thing about the apostle Paul, that somewhere or other he responded. They have written essays on it. How when he saw Stephen there, he must have thought, "Well, I've done wrong." But this is all conjecture. He was struck down by a vision of the Lord Jesus and was saved.

Now when someone goes forward at a rally and signs a decision card, and is gloriously saved, I well understand that they would have an emphasis that you have got to respond to God, to the call of God. But you see, we have got two ends of a truth that with our finite eyes we will never be able to fathom. But when you bring everybody together, we have a marvellous fullness. We do not have to be divided on such things. I mean, if you want to have a shindy [noisy disturbance, quarrel] about it, I can give you a few scriptures to start it straightaway on both sides! I have been in the business long enough to know just what those scriptures are. I remember years ago when I was an Arminian. I argued in that debate we had in Ismailia about it. Noel Hunt took my autographed book and he just put: "John 6:44—Think about it." It says, "All that the Father hath given Me shall come unto Me, and I will give them eternal life. And on the last day, I will raise them up." There could not be anything more conclusive than that, could there? No loss there. I remember thinking, "Well, he must be wrong." But over the years, I have journeyed right the way round, till I have come to see that that probably is the last word in the matter. That is why I firmly believe that Jewish people will be saved (see Romans 11:26) —because it is pure Calvinism. "The gifts and the calling of God are irrevocable" (see Romans 11:29). Paul said it in connection with that people.

So I am going to just say, why should we be divided on these things? Is the Lord not bigger than any of us? If we can stay together with these differences of emphasis, and yet see the place of one another, there is a fullness that comes into everything. We even have it in the Bible. Paul says, "You see that a man is saved by faith alone without works." While in the same generation, by the same Holy Spirit, James writes, "You see, that man is saved by faith, not by faith only, but by works also" (James 2:24). Of course, some people with their little Western minds think: "It blows my mind. I can't understand it, I can't get it." I do not think it is anything to worry about at all. I think they are saying the same thing, actually. But they see things from a different point of view. All I know is that in this mystery of Christ, there is James, and there is Paul, and they are going to be together forever.

In spite of the fact that Martin Luther saw so much in what the apostle Paul said, he could not accept James. He said the epistle of James was fit for nothing except for lighting a stove. Well, that is what has happened in church history. It is often not the first men, but what comes afterwards where we have all the fights.

Real Unity—Practically

What is the truth of this matter? It is that there is only one church. There is only one body because there was only one Christ. So, Christ is our oneness and the Holy Spirit is the custodian. Did you hear that? Christ is your oneness, my oneness, the oneness between us, and the Holy Spirit is the custodian of that unity. You remember the words of benediction at the end of II Corinthians chapter 13:14:

> *The grace of our Lord Jesus Christ, and the love of God,*
> *and the communion of the Holy Spirit, be with you all.*

Communion—or as it says in some of the modern versions, *fellowship* of the Holy Spirit—be with you all. The "sharing power" of the Holy Spirit be with you all. In other words, the Holy Spirit is the custodian of the oneness of Christ. He is the one that makes it a viable, dynamic matter. Instead of it being some theory, some ideal, it becomes a practical, viable, powerful reality. It is the Holy Spirit who breathes into us all in such a way that we realise how little we are, and how we need one another. It is the Holy Spirit who cuts us down to size in the most gracious manner, so that whoever we are, we realise we have not got everything; we need our brothers and sisters. That is why the Holy Spirit, the custodian of this unity, manifests Himself through whom He will He does not consult with elders or with congregation, He manifests Himself through whom He will, for the profit of all. Sometimes He takes the most humble person and gives them a word of knowledge. For those who are in leadership, it is sometimes quite hard to suddenly find that someone, who is quite unlettered, has got the key to a situation. Yet the Holy Spirit is the custodian of this unity, and it is as if He is saying, no single member is valueless. So, there are times when the Holy Spirit takes the most humble members, and through them, He gives the mind of God.

That is why I am so afraid of some of these pyramid structures, these great, top-heavy authoritarian structures. There *is* authority in the church. We *are* to obey them that have the rule over us. There *is* such a thing as covering. There *is* such a thing as submission. However, we have to be very, very careful of this kind of authoritarian structure where we get the mentality (and those who are in leadership and everybody else gets it) that they are the only ones who ever get the mind of God, that it is always up there that the mind comes. It does not always. In our history, we found again and again, that when we have been seeking the Lord, the Lord's mind has come through the most humble members. Then as we have taken it up, we have found the mind of God for us all together, because the Holy Spirit is the custodian of this unity. He does it in such a way that He balances the whole time.

Note very carefully that word in John 17. (I do not think it comes out in the Authorised Version, if I am right; it comes out in the Revised Version, and American Standard Version, and then all the modern versions afterwards.) In John chapter 17, starting in verse 21, then 22b, 23, the Lord Jesus said:

> *That they may all be one; even as thou, Father, art in me, and I in thee, that they also may be in us: that the world may believe that thou didst send me ... that they may be one, even as we are one; I in them, and thou in me, that they may be perfected into one.*

Now that is very interesting, is it not? *Perfected into one.* So first, our Lord says, "That they may be one; even as Thou art in Me, and I in Thee that they also may be in Us." That is an absolute unity—but in the next moment, He prays that they may be one, that they may be perfected into one. So, on the basis of an absolute unity, we are knit together. Is that not beautiful? You see, in Christian circles, we have put the second perfecting into unity, as the first matter. Do you get it? We have put the being perfected into unity, growing into unity, first, and the absolute unity as a goal. Whereas the Lord Jesus put it the other way around, the absolute unity is something we are born into. Then on the basis of that, in that by the Holy Spirit, we are perfected into one. I only pray that God gives you light on this and if you really go home and really pray about it and ask for it, He will.

You see, when you take a letter, like the Ephesian letter, you will find it starts to speak about how you may grow up into Christ, who is the head from whom all the body fitly framed and knit together through that which every joint supplies, and so on. Got it? So, we are in Him, but we have to grow up into Him.

We are in Him—that is the absolute—but now we have to be perfected.

Is that not our problem? Surely, that is our problem. It is lovely to be able to say, "We are all one. We are all one!" But when we come to it, we suddenly find that there are a lot of problems. Human beings being human beings, we have problems. Every human being is a problem. It is true! As someone said, "I like the world, but it's human beings that are the problem." Human beings are a problem. I am a problem to you; you are a problem to me. It is true. If we could only have this lovely theoretical unity, and all live at a distance, we would not have any problem. But it is when we have to work together, think together, plan together, act together, that we begin to rub up to one another the wrong way and then all of a sudden we ask, "What is there about this unity?" Now if we do not hold fast the unity which is ours in Christ, we cannot be perfected into one. It is only as we determine to maintain that unity of the Spirit that we can grow into one.

Now look very carefully at this manner. In Ephesians chapter four, you will find there the two kinds of unity. Look at chapter four of Ephesians and verse 13, where we are told this:

Till we all attain unto the unity of the faith, and of the knowledge of the Son of God, unto a full grown man.

Note the words "till we all attain unto the unity of the faith." The word is literally "and the full knowledge of the Son of God unto a full-grown man." That all speaks of a process, it all speaks of something progressive, something we are attaining to. As one version puts it beautifully, "till we all arrive at;" we are arriving at it. What have we to do whilst we are arriving at the unity of the faith? Ephesians 4:3:

Giving diligence to keep the unity of the
Spirit in the bond of peace.

In other words, what we have done in Christian circles is we have made the unity of the faith our basis and the unity of the Spirit, our goal; whereas the unity of the Spirit is our basis, and the unity of the faith is our goal. We do not see eye-to-eye yet—but we will. It says in the prophecy of Isaiah that then shall they see eye-to-eye in that day. The apostle Paul says, "those of us who are perfect are thus minded," have the same mind.

In other words, the more we grow up, the more real oneness we have because we can give ground for the smaller things. On the essentials, we stay together and go through together. Do you understand? I think it is important to see this because if we do not, we will never stay together. There will come issues that will tear you in two. There will come controversies in the world which will have its complement in the church. Then we shall all be at sixes and sevens. There is only one way through. I do not know whether we can ever be absolutely one on this matter of the unity of the faith till we are with the Lord. What a day that will be when the Lord says, "Now, this meant this, and this that" and when we suddenly see, "Oh, my!" I do not think any one of us will be 100% right. We will not be able to sit there sort of preening our feathers saying, "Oh! I was right! All the way through." I do not think any of us will be right. Would we not be sad if we made the unity of the faith a basis for division? Therefore, this whole matter is very important.

What then should be our practical attitude in this matter? Here we have got it in Romans 15:7:

Wherefore receive ye one another, even as Christ also received you, to the glory of God.

How did Christ receive you? Did He receive you as a marvellous 'going on' saint? Did He receive you as an elite overcomer? Did He receive you as a pure, sweet, spiritual virgin, unadulterated, unmixed, no impurity? The Lord Jesus did not receive any of us like that. How did He receive you? How did He receive me? He received you and me as sinners. He received us on the basis that you and I were no good and that He saved us through His finished work. Now, would it not be wonderful if we would receive one another one that basis? There is a minimal basis upon which I can receive you: you have been saved by the grace of God. But you know we do not do that, do we? When we look at one another, we do not mind receiving someone who has just been saved a few days ago on that basis. But as soon as it is beyond that we think: "So-and-So should pull their socks up. Why don't they get baptised? Time they got baptised. There's something wrong there. They'd been baptised a year ago if they've been hearing God." So we set about filling the lack. We leave little books about baptism around. We draw attention to it at every possible opportunity.

Sometimes it is a question of dress. We see somebody and say, "We don't like that dress. They're worldly!" Or something else. Because God has spoken to me, I feel He should speak to you. "God says I can't go to films. How can you? If I cannot go and see *Death on the Nile*, why you should go and see *Death on the Nile*? So what I'll do is I'll give you a 'straight to the jaw' spiritually on Sunday morning because I feel God has spoken to me. How come He hasn't spoken to you?" There is only one reason. If He says don't go that *Death on the Nile* ..." (now, I'm not saying He did say to me "Don't go to *Death on the Nile*." I know a whole lot of you will have a bad time! I know half of you were in that place watching that film. But you know what I mean.) Because God speaks to me, I feel, "What about him? What about her?" God says to you, "You shouldn't cut your hair short." So then immediately you say, "What about So-and-So?" God says, "... that lipstick." So immediately you say, "What about So-and-So? How come she can pray with those unclean lips?" It is a strange thing! You must remember that God may lead you a particular way because He is doing something in you. You have to go that way with Him. I know some people who could not play football or cricket. Now if God told me not to play cricket, it would not have meant a thing! It would never have meant a thing to me! It would have been no problem! I would have said, "Yes, Lord!" But if cricket has become an idol in somebody's life, and God says to them, "No more cricket," it does not mean that forever afterwards, there is no more cricket. But what it does mean is this: the Lord is trying that person. Are they obedient?

You see, the trouble with all of us is that anything God does in our lives, we make it a pattern for everybody else. If God did this in me, then I will say to you, "No matter that he took 10 years getting me to the place where I no longer smoke, that doesn't matter! I, by the grace of God, will get you through in half a year. I will give you little pamphlets on lung cancer. I will draw your attention to heart disease and to the fact that no temple of God should be defiled by smoke." We do this to one another, instead of receiving one another. Now, get me right on this. I am not saying that there is not sometimes a place for faithful fellowship, not a place sometimes for caring for one another. However, there is a vast difference when it is sharing something after there has been much prayer in your heart and much love and much concern. There is a vast difference between that and somehow bludgeoning another person through because God has said something to you, and therefore you think they should also follow the same way immediately.

"Receive ye one another as also Christ received you to the glory of God." If you look back in Romans 14:1, you will see exactly what it means because it says, "Him that is weak in faith, receive ye, yet not for decision of scruples." This is how it is rendered in mine, which is a terribly wordy rendering. But the rendering I always like best is: "not for investigation of his conscience." (I think it is the Revised Standard Version.) Do not investigate one another's conscience. Leave that to God. Love one another. Receive one another. Do not be partakers of one another's sins, but nevertheless, receive one another, care for one another and let God do the work.

You see, when it goes on in chapter 14 it says, "One man hath faith to eat all things: but he that is weak eateth herbs." Some would not feel that he that is weak eateth herbs. They would feel he that is strong eateth herbs—the vegetarian. But considering what the apostle Paul is saying, note this. Now I am putting this in modern terms now, rather than the religious terms of the old days, because in those days, it was a question of being kosher or non-kosher and it was a very big crisis in the early church. Those who were of Jewish background found it very hard to have a fellowship meal with those of Gentile background because of their kitchens, because of their hygiene standards, and all the rest of it and because of some of the things that the Gentiles ate. Well, you understand the same thing. I mean, some of you would go a bit green if you were asked to go to a meal and had to eat dog or horse! You would! You see, it is the same thing because that is not our culture. The Chinese eat dogs, very beautifully cooked, it is true. But I mean … I could not! Just supposing there is a Chinese family down the road that just got saved and they asked you to go and have a fellowship meal with them. Then they are having a specialty! You can see your stomach rolling already can you not? You think: "Oh, dear! I will have to make an excuse. I'll go have a cup of tea afterwards with them or something like that." Well, this was the same kind of thing really, but I have seen this matter of food become a problem.

There are those who feel food is impure, that there are so many things injected into meat, and so many things in our food and you know, they start and they say, "You know, that's poison." If you have white flour, it is poison; white sugar … oh, dear! Now, I am not saying you should not have brown sugar or that you should not be very careful about your diet, but do not let the way you feel about something become a means of division from your brothers and sisters. If someone is weak and feels all kinds of things are impure, and therefore it is better to keep off them, well, respect them. Do not let it be a means of division. You know, if we could only realise this, so many of the little things that destroy our unity would themselves be abolished.

Well, I think that is enough for now, but the mystery of Christ is the oneness of Christ in action. We as a company of God's people have seen this over the years, and by the grace of God we have practiced it. But I do pray with all my heart that we might be more into this matter in the years that lie ahead. It will require not only the old ones, it requires you younger ones as well. If you do not take a positive stand to see that the Lord Jesus is the oneness, then age will become a barrier, just as sex can become a barrier, or theological outlook can become a barrier, or anything else can become a barrier. Would it not be a marvellous thing if in the days that lie ahead, we were the oneness of Christ in action here in our town? That all those around us looking at us could see different colours, different nationalities, different racial backgrounds, different outlooks, different emphases, different temperaments, different ages, men and women, gloriously one because the Lord Jesus is the unity. That is the mystery. It has to be put to the concrete test here on Earth in time.

May the Lord give us help. Shall we pray?

Lord, there is not one of us who at some time or another has not sinned against another believer and Thou hast said that, Lord, if we do not forgive those that trespass against us, neither will You forgive us. Dear Lord, we pray that You will help us in this matter. Help us to see the whole question in its broader principles, to see what this unity is, the nature of it, how we are born into it, Lord. Illuminate our hearts. Let divine light shine into us from the youngest to the oldest, Lord, those who know this matter, Lord, let light shine in new ways, Lord.

Then we pray, Lord, Thou wilt help us that we may really be this oneness of the Lord Jesus in action, that there may be such a harmony and such a care for one another, such a growing up, such a complementing of one another, that, Lord, it will be just wonderful. Sweep away all those middle walls. They have gone, Father, through the finished work of the Lord Jesus. If in any way they have been rebuilt by our carelessness or ignorance, abolish them this night, we pray, through the power of the Holy Spirit, and may we flow together in the oneness of our Lord Jesus. This we ask in His precious Name. Amen.

5.
The Mystery Throughout the Ages

Ephesians 3:1–13

For this reason I, Paul, the prisoner of Christ Jesus for the sake of you Gentiles—Surely you have heard about the administration of God's grace that was given to me for you, that is, the mystery made known to me by revelation, as I have already written briefly. In reading this, then, you will be able to understand my insight into the mystery of Christ, which was not made known to people in other generations as it has now been revealed by the Spirit to God's holy apostles and prophets. This mystery is that through the gospel the Gentiles are heirs together with Israel, members together of one body, and sharers together in the promise in Christ Jesus. I became a servant of this gospel by the gift of God's grace given me through the working of his power. Although I am less than the least of all the Lord's people, this grace was given me: to preach to the Gentiles the boundless riches of Christ, and to make plain to everyone the administration of this mystery, which for ages past was kept hidden in God, who created all things. His intent was that now, through the church, the manifold wisdom of God should be made known to the rulers and authorities in the heavenly realms, according to his eternal purpose that he accomplished in Christ Jesus our Lord. In him and through faith in him we may approach God with freedom and confidence. I ask you, therefore, not to be discouraged because of my sufferings for you, which are your glory (NIV).

I would like to take up another matter to do with the practical relevance of this mystery of Christ to us all. The mystery of Christ is a tremendous term that is used, particularly in the New Testament in the letters of Paul. It is not just some luxury or some wonderful and glorious insight into something which is not so very relevant to us, and not so very practical. In actual fact, the mystery of Christ brings us to the very heart of God's purpose as to why He created the world, why He created man; why, when man fell, He persevered, what is the object of our salvation, and all these other things.

Last time, I began on the matter of the practical relevance to us all of the mystery of Christ. I said that it was the oneness of Christ in action. The heart of the mystery, this secret which God has communicated to all born again believers, is that we are one with Christ. We have been brought into a union with the Lord Jesus. Because we have become one with Him, we have become one with one another. As it says in Romans 12:5, we have become one body in Christ. We are not only one body *of* Christ, we become one body *in* Christ. That is, we are not only members of the Lord Jesus, we are members one of another. We have not only become limbs of Christ, parts of Christ (to put it literally using another English word) but we have become limbs or parts of one another. That is the intensely, direct relationship that we have come into, spiritually, through a new birth. In this oneness of Christ, the middle wall of partition is gone. It does not matter whether it is racial differences, national differences, social differences, theological differences, temperamental differences, the sex barrier, or the age barrier. It does not matter what it is, it has all been abolished, though not the actual things. If you are Chinese, you remain Chinese; if you are American, you remain American; if you are British, you remain British; if you are Jewish, you are still Jewish; if you are Gentile, you are still Gentile. In background, you remain the same, but in Christ, you are one new man. The cause of bitterness, the cause of division, the cause of alienation is gone. The wall of hostility has gone. Whether it is the men versus women, or women versus men, or whether it is the old versus the young, or the young versus the old, in Christ, the wall of hostility has been removed at tremendous cost and we have all been brought into this amazing oneness. We are in the same Lord Jesus, and the same Lord Jesus is in us. That is the oneness of Christ, and really, the mystery of Christ is oneness in action. In other words, somehow that has got to be seen.

The Mystery from all Ages

Now, I want to just underline another matter which lies at the root of a tremendous amount. You may not feel that it does so much when I begin. However, I think if you go away and pray about it and think about it, it will come home to you that this matter is of tremendous relevance and importance. The mystery of Christ spans the whole of time. That is a very simple thing to say. The mystery of Christ spans the whole of time. It lies at the heart of the purpose of God, and spans the whole of the ages—not only one age. That is where people make their mistake. It is not one age, but all the ages. It has been revealed in only one age, but the work was going on from the beginning. Have you got it? The work has been going on right from the beginning, but it has only been revealed to us in this age. For instance, take Ephesians 3:5, 9. This is what the apostle Paul said:

> *which in other generations was not made known unto the*
> *sons of men, as it hath now been revealed unto his holy*
> *apostles and prophets in the Spirit ... and to make all men*
> *see what is the dispensation [stewardship or administration]*
> *of the mystery which for ages hath been hid in God ...*

So, this mystery has been hidden in God for ages. It has not been revealed for ages and generations. Now, a biblical generation is 40 years. An age can be much, much longer. It can be a couple of thousand years or it can be a thousand years. But for ages and generations, this secret of the Lord has not been revealed; it has been hidden in God. Take again, Romans 16:25:

Now to him that is able to establish you according to
my gospel and the preaching of Jesus Christ, according
to the revelation of the mystery which hath been kept in
silence through times eternal, but now is manifested …

That is a marvellous phrase, is it not? "But hath now been revealed," it says, "but now is manifested." So, it has been kept in silence, for times eternal. Look at Colossians 1:26:

Even the mystery which hath been hid for ages and
generations: but now hath it been manifested to his saints.

Now, let us come back to this matter. Although it has been revealed in this age, the work began from the beginning. It did not commence with Pentecost. It did not even commence with the calling of the twelve apostles. It went right back to the first time that God took hold of a human being, and by their looking forward to the coming of the Messiah, saved them. Now, that is really when this began.

Every Born-Again Believer

Now let us put it in a little more forceful way, if we can. What does it mean? This oneness of Christ is not just a question of how all the believers who gather at Halford House ought to be one because the Bible says they should be one. It does not even mean that all the believers who live in Richmond ought to be one because the Bible says they are one. It does not even mean that all the believers alive at this present point in time in the whole world, whether Iran, or Afghanistan, or Saudi Arabia, or China, or behind the Iron Curtain, or in the New World, or here, ought to be one because the Bible says we are one. This oneness includes every truly saved human being, every born again believer in this age. Now, when you begin to think of that, it is really tremendous. It may seem to be a little more abstract to begin with, but we will come to that in just a moment. You see, what we are saying is that the apostle Paul was in this union with Christ. The apostle John was in this. The apostle Peter was in this. Timothy was in this. Barnabas was in this. Titus was in this. Later on, many others came into it. Jerome was in it. Saint Augustine was in it. Later, Martin Luther came into it. John Calvin was in it. Zwingli was in it. George Fox was in it, just to mention a few names that we know. John and Charles Wesley, and George Whitefield were in it. George Müller and J.N. Darby were in it. Watchman Nee was in it. Austin Sparks was in it. Mrs. Penn-Lewis was in it and today we are in it.

This unity is really a tremendous thing. Jesus said, "Neither for these only do I pray, but for those who believe on Thy name, that they may all be one; even as Thou, Father, art in Me, and I in Thee, that they also may be in Us" (see John 17:20–21). He was not thinking of a few people living together at a particular time in Richmond who gather at Halford House. Of course, it is included, but it is far bigger than that. He was praying for all those who would come after those twelve apostles. (Actually, it was eleven because remember He said, "the son of perdition, he was the only one I didn't keep because he's gone to his own end.") But He was praying for every single person after that, who would be saved by the grace of God, who should be born of the Spirit of God. He said, "that they may all be one; even as Thou, Father, art in Me, and I in Thee, that they may be in Us." This is the mystery of Christ. It means that every born again believer is in Christ, all born again believers are in Christ. Whether from the New Testament age, or since then, or now, we are all in the same marvellous unity. Look at Ephesians 2:19–22:

> So then ye are no more strangers and sojourners, but ye
> are fellow-citizens with the saints, and of the household
> of God, being built upon the foundation of the apostles
> and prophets, Christ Jesus himself being the chief corner
> stone; in whom each several building, fitly framed together,
> groweth into a holy temple in the Lord; in whom ye also
> are builded together for a habitation of God in the Spirit.

Now will you note this little word here: "So then ye are no more strangers and sojourners, but ye are fellow-citizens with the saints, and of the household of God." That is interesting: "... fellow citizens with the saints." What saints? Look at Hebrews 12:22–24:

> ... but ye are come unto mount Zion, and unto the
> city of the living God, the heavenly Jerusalem, and to
> innumerable hosts of angels, to the general assembly and
> church of the firstborn who are enrolled in heaven, and to
> God the Judge of all, and to the spirits of just men made
> perfect, and to Jesus the mediator of a new covenant.

Just Men Made Perfect

Now, just think of it, the writer says, "We have come to Mount Zion, we have come to the city of the living God, the heavenly

Jerusalem, to the innumerable hosts of angels, to the general assembly and church of the firstborn." Then he says, this amazing word, "to the spirits of just men made perfect." We have already come there. So, at any single point in which God brings us into the family of God, we come into something which He has been doing for the whole of this age, and there are already many who have been made perfect—men justified and brought to completeness. As I said previously, we have got to come to maturity. That is the whole point of this mystery: that we might grow up in Christ, we might come to the full-grown man, we might come to the full stature. Well, we are told we have already come there. We have come to this Mount Zion, we have come to this heavenly Jerusalem, we have come to this city of the living God, we have come to the spirits of just men made perfect, to Jesus, the mediator of this New Covenant.

Now take another scripture, 1 Thessalonians 4:16:

For the Lord himself shall descend from heaven, with a shout, with the voice of the archangel, and with the trump of God: and the dead in Christ shall rise first.

"The dead in Christ shall rise first." Now, you might wonder why I have read this particular verse. But just think: the dead—where? In Christ. Where are you? You are physically alive in Christ. They are even more alive in Christ. They are called the dead in Christ. They are actually more alive than we are. But is that not amazing? You are in Christ, and they are in Christ. You have come to this Mount Zion. You have come to this city of the living God. You have come to the heavenly Jerusalem. You have come to the spirits of just men made perfect. When the Lord comes to wind up this whole age, in fact, wind up the ages of time, then it says, "We which are alive and remain will in no way precede those who have fallen asleep in Jesus. But the dead in Christ shall rise first and then we which are physically alive in Christ will be caught up together with them and so shall we be forever with the Lord," and the whole mystery will be unveiled. This for all those who are joined to God's Messiah, all those who have been made alive to God through Him, all those who become members of His body, all those who have become living stones built together to be that holy temple in the Lord. I find it rather amazing.

The Church through the Ages

At present, again, you may not quite see why we are majoring on this point as something that has practical relevance to us, but you will see it in just one moment. The fact is this: there is only one church. There is not a New Testament church (as people often call it) and then a church in the Dark Ages, and then a Reformed Church and then a modern church or whatever you like to call it. There is only one church. It does not have any label. It is one church. There is only one church and there is only one body. How many bodies has the Lord Jesus got? He has only one body. Is that body only those who are physically alive today here on this earth? Of course not. Was not Paul a member of that body? Was not Peter a member of that body? Were not Luther and Calvin and Zwingli members of that body? Were John Wesley and Charles Wesley and George Whitefield members? Of course! There we understand, and we begin to see it! Now if they were members of that body, so are you. Now, it takes you right out of this humdrum routine, parochial little idea where we are all closed up to one another in some small little locality, shoved together, and it sometimes becomes very, very claustrophobic. We suddenly realise that our salvation is tremendous. We have been introduced into something which was in the heart of God from before time began. It was in His heart when He created the universe, when He created human beings. Even when they fell, it was in His heart in redemption. Then when the Saviour came, it was in the Saviour's heart, right from the beginning.

So, by the grace of God, you and I have come into this one body of the Lord Jesus. Is it not marvellous? I cannot think of anything more marvellous. I sometimes think of how it has been my privilege to have known great saints. I thank God that I ever knew Austin-Sparks. I thank God that I had the privilege of knowing Lady Ogle. I thank God for many dear brothers and sisters I have known personally. I thank God I have this privilege. It is a great joy to me to think how I am in the same thing they were in. I am so unworthy and yet I am a fellow-member with them, of the body of the Lord Jesus.

But think! Do you realise that in the body you are in, you are a fellow-member with the apostle Paul, and you are a fellow-member with Peter and John and James? Do you realise that you are a fellow-member with people like Augustine and Jerome? You are a fellow-member with Luther and Zwingli and Calvin and Wesley and George Fox and all the others. It is tremendous! Think of the privilege! Is it not a marvellous thing to be saved? It is an absolutely amazing thing. You might think to yourself, "I am just an unknown. I mean, just a few people here know my name, who else knows my name?" Do you know, I myself do not doubt that the apostle Paul knows your name. It would seem a very strange thing to me, this cloud of witnesses, if they do not know the names of all those who are being added. I bet they go (if I may so use a Sunday school term) every day to look at the register of those being added. Do not forget that for them this is the secret of everything. I mean, this is what lies at the heart of the whole thing.

We have been praying about Iran and Afghanistan—think of all the unrest and hostility. It is going to grow and grow and grow as we come to the climax of the age and the coming of the Messiah. Those who have passed on, if they are at all conscious in the presence of the Lord, must know that this is the heart of the whole matter! This is the thing that was in the heart of God from the beginning! Every single one is a fellow-member with us and is very precious to us. If we get a love for the people of God, so that somehow or other they become precious to us, then we want to get to know them, we want to know their name, we want to get to know who they are. How much more must it be for those who have borne so much of the responsibility on their shoulders? We are all going to be together forever; we are not going to be one great anonymous mass. Somehow or other, there is going to be a getting to know one another. Well, I find it rather wonderful when you think of it like that. There is only one church, there is only one body, there is only one bride, there is only one city and that is the mystery of Christ. The heart of it all is union with Christ.

The Communion of the Saints

Now, we do not say the Apostles' Creed here, and I have often been sorry that we do not. I think it would be a very good thing now and again, to go back to that old confession of the creed together. Not because we want to put our faith in some written document, but because now and again, the simple statement of elementary, essential, and fundamental truth is a great help in the very unseen. One of the things we say in the Apostles' Creed, which is the oldest creed, and the simplest of all that goes right back to the third century of the church is this: "I believe in the communion of saints." Do you remember that, those of you who have got a more Anglican background? "I believe in the communion of saints." What does it mean? Did you think it meant, "I believe in fellowship"? Well, of course it meant fellowship, and it means a good deal more than just you and somebody else getting to know each other in the Lord. "I believe in the communion of saints." The *comm-union* of saints—the whole practical entity of those who were born of God. It is not many circles; it is only one circle. It is not many families, only one family. It is not many communions, only one communion.

People sometimes speak of denominations as a communion. I sometimes hear people say, "I belong to such and such a communion," and someone else says, "I belong to such and such a communion." Well, there is the communion, *the* communion of saints, and there is only one communion. It is one glorious communion that consists of every single born again believer. Now, I think that is something to get quite excited about. I do not think that many Christians would ever confess that, because their horizons are much narrower. They say, "I believe in fellowship." We believe in fellowship; we feel strongly about it. We believe that most people should have fellowship, but it is much bigger than that. This fellowship comprises all those whom God has gathered into the Lord Jesus.

"I believe in the communion of saints." There will be some in there we will be a bit surprised about and there will be some notable absentees. Just because a person had a collar, or a title, or a position does not mean they are in the communion of saints and just because some people had some rather weird ideas does not mean that they are not in it. It is strange. Yet, only God knows the elect and everyone who has been born of the Spirit, is in this communion.

Now, I would like to take it a step further because this may clear up some problems you may have on some issues. It may or it may not. It is clear from the Word of God that all the Old Testament saints are in this communion. Some people do not think so. They think we can do without the Old Testament. "The Old Testament is like someone's appendix," they used to say. "It is prehistoric; something left over from prehistoric days where men went around chewing on more meat and bones. They had an appendix, you see. It's useless to us today." (That is what they used to say.) People look upon the Old Testament that way. They say, "Ah, the Old Testament, it is prehistoric! They used to go around slaughtering one another in the name of the Lord. I mean, it doesn't mean anything to us today. It is just those dark days when people were very poor and hardly literate and ..."

Fellow-Heirs

Just wait! What does it mean in Ephesians? The trouble is that we read these scriptures, but they never come home to us! Listen to Ephesians 3:4–6: "... the mystery of Christ, which in other ages and generations has not been shown ... to wit, that the Gentiles are fellow-heirs," listen, "and fellow-members of the body, and fellow-partakers of the promise." I do like the way it is put here. I think it is much clearer in this New International Version. I like it very much: "The mystery is that through the gospel, the Gentiles are heirs together with Israel, members together of one body, and sharers together in the promise in Christ Jesus."

"Fellow-heirs" with whom? Fellow-heirs with the saints in the Old Covenant! Must be, must it not? Fellow-members of the body! "Oh, do you mean they were in the body? But they can't have been because the body wasn't revealed then?" You are quite right. That is the mystery which was not revealed, but it does not mean they were not in the spiritual entity. Do you understand? They were in the spiritual entity though it had not been revealed to them.

"Fellow-partakers of the promise." It does not say—get this clear, because we are all so big headed—it does not say "they are fellow-heirs with us, fellow-members of the body with us, fellow-partakers in the promise in Christ Jesus with us." No, we are fellow-heirs with them. We are fellow-members of the body with them. We are fellow-partakers of the promise with them. The shoe is on the other foot.

Fellow-Citizens

Now just take another little thing, just to make sure you understand this. Look at Ephesians 2:19:

> So then ye [this is Gentiles] are no more strangers and
> sojourners, but ye are fellow-citizens with the saints.

Who was he talking about when he wrote this in the first century? What saints? Fellow-citizens with the saints, he meant the Old Testament saints! Is that not amazing? Now let us go a little bit further with this matter. Look at Ephesians 2:12:

> that ye were at that time separate from Christ,
> alienated from the commonwealth of Israel, and
> strangers from the covenants of the promise ...

I like that. Here it is in the New International Version, which I also like very much. This is how it is put:

> remember that at that time you were separate from
> Christ, excluded from citizenship in Israel and
> foreigners to the covenants of the promise ...

The Same Kingdom

> And I say unto you, that many shall come from the east and
> the west, and shall sit down with Abraham, and Isaac, and
> Jacob, in the kingdom of heaven: but the sons of the kingdom

shall be cast forth into the outer darkness: there shall be the
weeping and the gnashing of teeth (Matthew 8:11–12).

Is that not interesting? He says, about these that are going to be saved, they shall come from the North and South, from the East and the West and they shall sit down in the kingdom with Abraham, Isaac, and Jacob. So, it is the same kingdom. You see, there is the little phrase that is often used wrongly, in my estimation, by many. It is that little phrase that the Lord Jesus said about John the Baptist, "He that is least in the kingdom of heaven is greater than he." People have therefore taken it that the Lord Jesus was saying all the Old Testament saints were really pathetic, spiritually. That the least, and most insignificant, and most unworthy born again believer under the New Covenant is of greater spiritual character and worth than them. However, I do not think so at all. He was not saying this is the kingdom and that is not the kingdom; the born again believers in the New Covenant are in the kingdom, but the others are not. What He was saying is this: that the least in the kingdom of God under the New Covenant has greater privileges and advantages than even John the Baptist. Otherwise, why do we talk about being fellow-citizens with them, fellow-partakers with them, fellow-heirs with them if they are so little, so pathetic?

But listen, there is a good deal more than this. It is rammed home in other things. Look at Luke 13:28–30:

There shall be the weeping and the gnashing of teeth, when
ye shall see Abraham, and Isaac, and Jacob, and all the
prophets, in the kingdom of God, and yourselves cast

forth without. And they shall come from the east and
west, and from the north and south, and shall sit down
in the kingdom of God. And behold, there are last who
shall be first, and there are first who shall be last.

Or again, Revelation 21:12:

... having a wall great and high; having twelve gates, and at
the gates twelve angels; and names written thereon, which
are the names of the twelve tribes of the children of Israel.

So the names of the twelve patriarchs are on the twelve gates of the bride of Christ, the city of God. This heavenly Jerusalem, this city of the living God has twelve gates, and on the gates are the names of the twelve tribes of the children of Israel. Now look at verse 14:

And the wall of the city had twelve foundations, and on
them twelve names of the twelve apostles of the Lamb.

I cannot think that there could be anything clearer than this. You have the twelve patriarchs and you have the twelve apostles representing those of the elect people of God under the Old Covenant, and those, the elect people of God under the New Covenant. They are joined together in the one bride, the wife of the Lamb. I think this mystery is something worth beginning to think about if it is as wonderful as this.

You say to me, "Do you mean to tell me that that this goes back to Abraham?" Yes. "Do you mean to tell me that although

I'm a Gentile, totally a Gentile, I have been introduced into something which goes right back to Abraham, Isaac and Jacob?" Yes, you have. That is the glory of it. That is the wonder of it, this union with Christ. Supposing we used another word that would just put it into its Hebrew context. Supposing we said, "union with the Messiah." Our concept immediately begins to change! Immediately, there is an adjustment. Union with the Messiah! That is what they looked for. Abraham rejoiced to see His day. The gospel was preached to Abraham. So, Abraham, Isaac, Jacob, they all looked at that day. Moses looked at that day; he remembered, "A prophet like unto me shall the Lord your God raise. Him, shall you harken to," and so on. It is rather wonderful when you begin to see it like this.

Let me give you another scripture, the final punchline. Hebrews 11:8, 10:

> *By faith Abraham, when he was called, obeyed to go out unto a place which he was to receive for an inheritance; and he went out, not knowing whither he went ... for he looked for the city which hath the foundations, whose builder and maker is God.*

Abraham never did live in a city. He never lived in Jerusalem of this earth. He never lived in a city. All his life he lived in tents, yet, he looked for *the* city which has the foundations, whose builder and maker, or architect, is God. Dear Abraham. When we come to Revelation 21, we find somehow, that is the city which has the foundations, and the foundations had the twelve names, not of his great-grandsons but the names of twelve apostles.

Now turn in the same chapter to Hebrews 11:13–16:

These all died in faith, not having received the promises,
but having seen them and greeted them from afar, and
having confessed that they were strangers and pilgrims on
the earth. For they that say such things make it manifest
that they are seeking after a country of their own. And
if indeed they had been mindful of that city from which
they went out, they would have had opportunity to
return. But now they desire a better country, that is, a
heavenly: wherefore God is not ashamed of them, to be
called their God; for he hath prepared for them a city.

That is Abraham, Isaac, Jacob, Sarah, Rebecca, Rachel and Leah.
They are all included. Now go on. Verse 39, here we come to it.
Listen very carefully.

And these all ...

Who are these all? Go right back and you will find they are all
here. Going right back to Abel, Enoch, Noah, and then Abraham,
Isaac, Jacob, and their wives. Then on: Moses, Joshua, even Rahab
is here. She was a Gentile. Rahab the Egyptian, she is here.
Then we go on: Gideon, Barak, Samson, Jeptha, David, Samuel,
and the prophets. Now listen:

And these all, having had witness borne to them
through their faith, received not the promise.

Did you hear? Received not the promise. "The mystery of Christ,
to wit, that you are fellow-heirs, fellow-members of the body

and fellow-partakers in the promise through Christ Jesus." Now listen here. "Received not the promise." Now listen: "God, having provided some better thing concerning us. That apart from us, they should not be made perfect." That transforms everything, does it not? You should underline it. Apart from us. Apart from us, they should not be made perfect. So dear Abraham, Isaac, Jacob, Moses, these prophets, they cannot come to perfection. They cannot come to completion. They cannot come to full growth ... without us! So much for that idea that when the Jewish people rejected and crucified their Messiah, God had to think again and He thought up the church, a kind of secondary purpose. He brought in something because the people, His people failed and so He thought, "Now what shall I do?" Then He thought, "Yes. I'll, get the Gentiles in." No! from the very beginning it was His thought to have the Gentiles in. Only instead of it coming through the faithfulness of the Jewish people, it came through their fall. Instead of it coming through the "success" of the Jewish people, it came through their failure and their loss. Do you understand?

The Fullness of the Gentiles and All Israel

Now, let me just insert something here that may be a shaft of light for some people. The apostle Paul says (in Romans 11:12), that if the fall of the Jewish people is the riches of the world, and their loss, the riches of the Gentiles, how much more their fullness? If you have come into the unsearchable riches of the Messiah through the loss to the Jewish people, what will happen when they come to fullness? Verse 15:

For if the casting away of them [the Jewish people]
is the reconciling of the world, what shall the
receiving of them be, but life from the dead?

Many believers, I suspect, are like square pegs in round holes. You can study theology, you can study the Word, and yet have no understanding of the will of God for our day and generation.

This mystery of Christ is so tremendous. Because you see, God has been doing one thing from the beginning, not many things, one thing. In the wisdom of God, it has been achieved, not through the success of the Jewish people but through their fall. Do you think that He will then throw them away? No, the Scripture says:

For I would not, brethren, have you ignorant of this
mystery ... a hardening in part hath befallen Israel,
until the fulness of the Gentiles be come in; and so
all Israel shall be saved ... (Romans 11:25–26).

This does not mean just all the physical Jewish people, but it does mean that at the end, a tremendous number of Jewish people will be regathered back into the Israel of God. The natural branches will come back in when God has achieved His purpose. Now, do not get the civil service idea that suddenly one day, as it were, in heaven He says, "Now then, we've got the Gentiles in. No more Gentiles, now the Jews." Not at all. There will be a tremendous overlapping, but it will come.

This mystery of Christ, which has been in the heart of God from the very beginning, this matter of union with Him, has yet to have its last stages and phases fulfilled. So, my point is this: What a tremendous thing it is to know where we are in the economy of God. What a wonderful thing it is to know where we are! We should not just be wandering around in some kind of morass where we have all kinds of Biblical ideas, knowing that there should be evangelism, knowing that there should be teaching, and knowing that there should be prayer, but having no clue as to where we are in the economy of God.

I think the apostle Peter had a little bit of a clue do you not? He was the apostle to whom was given the key to open the door to the Gentiles. Remember the vision he had? There must have been something in his head and heart because of the way he preached on the day of Pentecost, and again a few days later when he said that God had done this amazing thing and was bringing people to Himself. Then he had that vision when he was on the roof in Joppa, when he saw all those things that were unclean. I suppose at the beginning, he did not quite understand it, but when he had to go up to Cæsarea to stay in a Gentile household, he knew full well what it meant. He had said, "I'd never eat anything that's not kosher." But he had to, I suppose, for a week or two. He must have stayed in Cæsarea and eaten their food and enjoyed fellowship at their tables with those people who found the Lord in the end. In those meetings, the key was put into the lock, and it was turned, and the door opened and the Gentiles came into the house of God.

So at the end of the age, I do not know how, but perhaps in a totally Jewish context, there will be a key put into the door, no drama about it, and suddenly, the door will be opened. From that moment, thousands and thousands of Jews will start to come back into their own olive tree. Now, their own olive tree is the mystery of Christ. He is the root and stem of Jesse. So, He is both, as it were, the foundation and the top stone. He is everything—heart and circumference.

Now, I have said that about the Old Testament saints as an aside so that it gives you a little better idea of perhaps what sometimes we are so burdened about. This which we are in, we tend to think of as something so totally Gentile in culture and in every way—but it is not Gentile in origin. It goes back to Abraham and, although over these two-thousand years God has worked to bring in people from every tongue, kindred and nation, those who are saved through His grace, born of His Spirit into the union with Christ, still it is the root that bears the branches and not the branches that bear the root. We must remember that. At the end, we are going to see this marvellous completion of the whole thing: "So shall all Israel be saved."

A Deliverer

Then you had that wonderful little word there, which is to me, so exciting. I must be careful of it because one can start to sort of get into total digression, but it says, "Even as it is written, 'There shall come out of Zion the deliverer; He shall turn away ungodliness in Jacob'" (Romans 11: 26). Now this is so interesting, because it is a quotation of a prophecy in Isaiah 59:20:

> And a redeemer shall come to Zion, and unto
> them that turn from transgression in Jacob.

That is the Hebrew. That is exactly what Jesus did. He came to Zion to those that turned from transgression in Jacob. That was the 11 apostles. It was the 120 in the upper room. It was the 3,000 on the day of Pentecost. It was the 5,000 a few weeks later. It was all those who turned in Judea and in Samaria. They turned from transgression in Jacob; they were Jews. But when the apostle Paul quotes this, he quotes the Septuagint version and there is a most marvellous change. I think it is all under the ordering of God. Instead of saying, "and the Redeemer shall come to Zion, unto them that turn from ..." it says:

> There should come out of Zion the deliverer and He
> shall turn away ungodliness from Jacob. And this is my
> covenant unto them, when I shall take away their sins.

So, when you come to Zechariah 12:10, where it speaks about the pouring out of the Spirit of grace and supplication, we naturally say, "Oh, when did that happen?" We are not quite sure. But then we have come to chapter 13:1:

> In that day there shall be a fountain open ... for uncleanness.

Then people get terribly muddled because they go on to Zechariah 13:6 and it says, "What are these wounds that are between your hands, in the midst of your hand?" They say, "This must be Jesus," but they do not understand that the work of the Lord Jesus actually spans the whole of Jewish history. So that the beginning of the church was those that turned from transgression in Jacob, to whom the Redeemer came and started all this that was to go out to the Gentiles and bring in all the Gentiles. But at the end, out of Zion—that is out of the spiritual Zion—shall come forth a deliverer, the Redeemer. In other words, then the Lord having done a work within all those He has brought in from the Gentiles into His Zion, there, He shall turn back to the Jewish people. Just like Joseph revealed himself to his brethren. Then, in that day, the fountain you and I have known, in which we have washed away all our sins, that fountain, that same fountain will be, as it were, opened to the house of Israel. It does not mean all Jews will be saved any more than the fullness of the Gentiles means all Gentiles will be saved. What it does mean is that every born again believer will be. All the elect people of God, amongst Jew and Gentile, will be saved. Thank God for that! I think that is worth knowing. I think it is worth realising that the mystery of Christ encompasses that.

Historical Continuity

Now, let us close this particular point. If you followed me, there is therefore a historical continuity in the work of God. In this matter of the mystery of Christ, there is a historical continuity. It goes right back to Pentecost and it includes all that God has done in the last 1900 and so many more years. It goes back even farther. It goes right the way back to the Old Covenant, right the way back to Abraham, who is the father of all those who believe.

Now, it is an understanding of this that is a corrective to localism, parochialism, and the mentality that everything has failed in church history but us. "We are the new beginning!" Oh, I have heard so many things; I travel around and I see all kinds of things. I also get letters, and I remember some years ago getting a letter from somebody who said, "You must come to us.

We will send you the air ticket, if you will only say that you will come. This is the first time in 112 years of American history that the Holy Spirit has moved." I knew instantly that the thing must fall to pieces. You cannot possibly make claims like that. You know the idea is: "Everything else has failed, but now ... we will not. We are God's new opportunity. We are the opportunity God has been looking for; we will not fail. Somehow or other we are all going to go through," and we cut ourselves off from it [the historical continuity]. It is nonsense; as if everything that has gone before has somehow collapsed.

It is true that every movement of the Holy Spirit has, within a generation or two, crystallised, formalised and become a monument to something that happened in the past. It does not mean that God does not save in such things, or does not bless in such things, and does not break in in such things. He does! Thank God for that! But so much that is denominational is now a monument for something that happened hundreds of years ago. We speak the language that they spoke, we sort of act as they acted, we often have the organisation that they had then, sometimes we even have the dress that they had then. It is as if somehow, God did something and we cannot go beyond it. It is as if we get frozen. We have to stay there when God did it. So, what was contemporary dress then, becomes, with each succeeding year, old-fashioned, until, in the end, it becomes the garb of our ministry—what was, at the time, a completely contemporary way of dressing. The language is suddenly frozen as if it is somehow spiritual. It is interesting, is it not?

What I am trying to get at is this: the moment any company, any house group, any movement of the Spirit in any part of the world or in any time in history think that they are it ... it is finished. As if somehow or other it has got everything. I have gone to groups where, for instance, they will never sing a hymn from the past because that is a closed book. "We have nothing to learn from the past; God is doing something with us." You know the kind of thing? "We are it." It is an outlet which cuts us off from all that has passed before. My point is this: We create much serious problem when we despise church history and ignore our rich heritage. Is it not obvious that if there is only one body, only one church, only one bride, only one city, what God has been doing in each successive generation must have real value for us and is it not true that it has?

What real believer questions justification by faith? Yet, when Luther first spoke about justification by faith, the whole world blew up. People went around saying, "What kind of crank is this man? He's a drunk. He likes his beer too much!" Everyone said, "You must be very careful of that man." Now, no one says, "Oh, be careful! Be careful! What a dangerous doctrine is justification by faith. Oh!" We all know it. I mean, we know it so well, we do not understand it. It is so much kindergarten business. We do not even inquire. We do not ask the Lord for revelation. "Well, we all understand that. That's kindergarten stuff. That's elementary." Half our neuroses come because of a failure to understand justification. Much of the accusation that the enemy uses to get a real hold in our lives comes because we do not understand justification. When we are in the battle with the forces of darkness, if we do not understand justification, we are knocked out. Well, I mean, we all agree; that is the point.

Then there are lots of other things. You know, when John Wesley began to talk about being born again, about new birth, it was as if the whole world just blew up. In the Anglican Church, they called them "enthusiasts" and said, "It is disgraceful; you were born again when you were baptised. There is no such thing as being born again, born anew like a second birth when you actually knew it." Then Wesley sort of committed the unpardonable by saying you should feel it. He actually said it, and you should think that was anathema to the Puritans. He sings of it in hymns! "I feel the blood." Have you ever noticed that in the Wesleyan hymns? That *feeling*? "I feel a fire glowing within me ..." There is a lot of feeling in the Wesleyan hymns. He did not, of course, mean soulish feeling. He meant a real knowledge that we are born again, the witness of the Spirit within.

I do not think that there are many believers all around the world who do not accept new birth today. We know we must be born again. We know it must be an experience. You cannot just be converted in the head. You must be born of the Spirit. You see, it has become ours. This is all part of our heritage. We who believe in baptism by immersion, we forget that the Anabaptists were trussed up in sacks—men, women and children—and dumped in fountains and rivers and lakes. We forget that thousands upon thousands were martyred, not just by Catholics, but by Protestants also. But today, this matter of believer's baptism is the most widely and commonly accepted form of baptism.

When the Brethren first started to meet together, they said, "We don't want any label; we want just to meet in Christ." I think we understand that more today. The Pentecostals talked about gifts. Oh, what a storm it must have been in the early part of the last century! In the middle of the 18th century, oh the storm there was over the Irvingites and they did get into excess. But oh, the storm over them, just because they dared to say that some of the things in the book did not die out with the church of the New Testament but are ours today. When A.B. Simpson dared to say that he believed that Christ could be the healer of the body. Dear A.B. Simpson ... what a storm! But we accept most of it now.

This is our heritage. Do you not see what I am trying to say? It is our heritage! Should we cut ourselves off as if God can only show *us* something new? No, of course not. Or this: there were people who were hounded out of this country to Holland, and then from Holland to the States, simply because they saw the truth of the independence of each congregation. There were others who died and were persecuted simply because they saw that elders were the right form of church government. Shall we just close the door on all this and say, "No, no, no, no, no! That's all old hat!" At the time, all that revelation was contested by Satan. In most cases, it was sealed with the blood of martyrs. It is our heritage.

What I am saying is that this mystery of Christ, this matter of spanning the whole of time is something tremendous because we have come in at the end. We might feel it would be rather marvellous to be at the beginning—everything fresh, everything new, everything growing—but we have come in at the end. I think it is even more marvellous, because we have got all this richness behind us. So, if we are able to think about the local nature or the current expression of this mystery of Christ, that fact must never take away from this other fact that it spans the whole of time. We want to be contemporary. We want it to be a local, concrete expression, through flesh and blood people, speaking contemporary language, dressing in contemporary clothes, living a contemporary life. But oh, we want to have that timeless and heavenly nature of the mystery as well. I think that lifts us out of a lot of traps, and keeps us from a lot of snares. May God help us in this matter.

Dear Lord, we just pray that Thou would somehow bring this home to us in a way that perhaps has never come home to us before. It is very easy, Lord, to somehow feel that we are involved in something which is just local, something petty and somehow just bounded by our own little lives. Lord, we pray that Thou would open our eyes to see what it is that Thou hast brought us into. Then one day when that whole building, that bride of yours, that wife of the Lamb, that city of God is unveiled, what a marvel it will be, Lord! We see that it will span all the ages and the whole of time and the marvel of it all will be that, Lord, we are there by Thy grace. Help us therefore, Lord, when we take this in conjunction with some of these other things, to see why we need to be built together and why we need to be subject to discipline and why we need, Lord, to have our own inner original experience of Thee. Help us, Lord, in these things and we ask it all in the name of our Lord Jesus.

6.
The Local Nature of Its Expression

Romans 16:25–27

Now to him that is able to establish you according to my gospel and the preaching of Jesus Christ, according to the revelation of the mystery which hath been kept in silence through times eternal, but now is manifested, and by the scriptures of the prophets, according to the commandment of the eternal God, is made known unto all the nations unto obedience of faith: to the only wise God, through Jesus Christ, to whom be the glory for ever. Amen.

Shall we bow together just in a word of prayer?

Lord, we want now very simply to commit this study to Thee. We know, Lord, that it can be just a lecture, but we pray that we may be delivered from it being only that. We pray, Lord, rather that Thou wilt take Thy Word and make it live to us, Lord. Give us that spirit of wisdom and revelation in the knowledge of the Lord Jesus. Cause the eyes of our hearts, Lord, to be enlightened that we may know Him in a deeper, clearer, fuller way than ever before. Lord, there are all kinds of facets of truth that maybe have not come home to us. We pray, Lord, that in Thine own wonderful way, Thou wilt cause us to see light in Thy light and oh, Lord, let the Word of Christ dwell in us richly in all wisdom. Grant that there may be a consequence and a result from this study. For we ask it in the name of our Lord Jesus, amen.

We come now to the last of these studies on this subject of *The Mystery of Christ*. As I have said, this little phrase the mystery of Christ does not mean mystery, as is so often understood today in the contemporary use of the word—something which we cannot understand or which is not communicated, which is not revealed. With this word the "mystery" of Christ, or the "mystery" of God, the Bible always uses words such as *is manifested, is revealed, is communicated.* In other words, the way the Holy Spirit has used this word mystery is of a secret which God communicates to those who are born of His Spirit. If that really is so, then what a tremendous privilege is ours as born again believers to really understand what it is that God has hidden for generations and ages, but has now revealed to His own in this age. It is tremendously important that you and I should come into an understanding of it.

Of course, we have a little of it in Ephesians 3:4–6:

> *... whereby, when ye read, ye can perceive my understanding*
> *in the mystery of Christ; which in other generations was*
> *not made known unto the sons of men, as it hath now*
> *been revealed unto his holy apostles and prophets in*

the Spirit; to wit, that the Gentiles are fellow-heirs, and
fellow-members of the body, and fellow-partakers of
the promise in Christ Jesus through the gospel ...

Now, in previous chapters we have introduced the subject, where we have had one whole chapter on "What is the Mystery of Christ," another on "The Challenge Inherent in the Revelation of that Mystery," and we have now spent two chapters on the subject of its practical relevance to us. We have considered, for instance, its practical relevance to us on earth, in time, in place, as being the oneness of Christ in action, because basically the mystery of Christ is union with Christ. You and I, by the grace of God, have been brought into a union with the Lord Jesus. Therefore, if by the grace of God, because of the Lord Jesus and you and the Lord Jesus and me, we have become one, then something has happened to us. We have not only become members of the Lord Jesus, of Christ, we have become members one of another. That is an amazing thing, is it not?

So, we have spent time considering this oneness—that the middle wall of partition has been destroyed. The barriers that divide us, whether age barriers, sex barriers, denominational barriers, racial barriers, national barriers, colour barriers or social barriers, they have all been abolished. This does not mean that we cease to be the nationality that we were born into, or that we cease to be the sex that we were born with, or that we cease to be the age that we actually are. Rather, those causes that divide us, those things that become the cause of bitterness and alienation and division or distance, those things have been abolished in our Lord Jesus and by His finished work.

Now, in the last study we talked about that little phase in the Apostles' Creed (for those of you who have ever known it, or recited it) in which we say, "I believe in the communion of saints." We talked about the simple fact that the whole people of God are *in Christ*, the Bible speaks of the dead *in Christ*, as well as those of us who are alive on earth as being *in Christ*. There is this marvellous union and communion. Of course, it does not mean we become spiritists, that we get messages from those who are dead, or that we try to contact them in any way. That is forbidden. What we do know is that we are in a glorious unity. This mystery of Christ, this church of Christ, this body of the Lord Jesus is not something which is just located in a particular period of time, but covers the whole of time. It is not only those under the New Covenant, but it goes right back to the beginning to Abraham and even before. That is rather wonderful, is it not? Now, I will not say any more about those matters.

Now, I would like to take two matters, both of which are vital. They really are vital. We can talk until we are blue in the face about being the church of Jesus Christ. We can talk endlessly about being the body of the Lord Jesus, but in the end, it is not theology that counts. In the final analysis, it is whether the Holy Spirit commits Himself. You can have all the Bible pattern in the world, you can have the most biblical pattern, you can have a New Testament pattern, but if the Holy Spirit does not commit Himself, it never becomes a living, organic, viable unity. It never becomes an organism. It never becomes something which is alive in God, growing in God, functioning by the power of God, achieving the ends of God. It cannot be unless the Holy Spirit commits Himself.

Therefore, these matters we are talking about are not just interesting theories or interesting ideals. They are in fact, absolutely essential. Unless we all learn how to maintain the unity of the Spirit, there will be no body of the Lord Jesus to function. If we make the ground of fellowship less than Christ, if we cut out some, who for one reason or another we feel do not see eye-to-eye with us although they are in Christ, immediately we have destroyed any effective building up of the church. If on the other hand, we add more than Christ, we do exactly the same. So, these things are very important.

The Local Nature of its Expression

Now, the first matter I would like to take up is the local nature of its expression. We have talked about the fact that this is a unity. It is the same unity as exists between the Father and the Son. Jesus said, "I pray for them, that they may be one, even as Thou Father art in Me and I in Thee, that they may be in Us" (John 17:21). That is not an organised unity. It is not a structural unity. It is an organic unity. No one has ever been able to define the unity of the Father, and the Son, and the Holy Spirit. It is an organic, essential, substantial unity. It is into *that* unity, that you and I are born by the Spirit of God.

Now, this unity has, and must have, a local expression. Let us look at this a little more; it sounds terribly technical to begin with. This church of God, this union with Christ, this body of which He is the head, this temple of the Lord, this home of God in the Spirit, has got to have a local expression. It has to be expressed in time, on earth, and in a given place. For instance, turn to Colossians 2:1–2:

> For I would have you know how greatly I strive for you
> [Colossians], and for them at Laodicea and for as many
> as have not seen my face in the flesh; that their hearts
> may be comforted, they being knit together in love, and
> unto all riches of the full assurance of understanding, that
> they may know the mystery of God, even Christ ...

So, the apostle's great concern is not that this be some mystical, ethereal, abstract, ideal, or truth that is very wonderful, a form of escapism, which helps us above the sort of normal humdrum routine. His great concern is that the people of God at Colossae and the people of God at Laodicea might really come right into this and know the mystery of God in experience—know the Lord Jesus; know Him, not only personally, but know Him corporately. It has got to be expressed, this union with the Lord Jesus, in time and in place.

Let me put it this way: this glorious and divine oneness with Christ has to be expressed *where* we live and *when* we live on this earth. Why do I say that? First of all, where we live, that is obvious. I mean, it is all very well to talk about some wonderful communion of saints, some invisible church, the body of the Lord Jesus comprised of all truly born again believers. But in the final analysis, it has to be expressed. It can just be a marvellous escapist theory. "Up there, everything is one. Up there, everything is without spot or blemish. Up there, everything is perfect." It has to come down to where we live. I cannot talk about being the church or belonging to the Lord Jesus if, in fact, I am in collision with my Christian brothers and sisters in the place where I live. That is where it is put to the test.

Then you form this other idea that this whole mystery of Christ is something really all to do with the ages to come. When we have died, or when the Lord has come, and we are changed in the twinkling of an eye, then this will all be a marvellous reality. Well, that is true. It will be a manifested reality, a publicly manifested reality. However, the work that ensures that you and I are in it has to be done now, here in time, and in a given place. In other words, it has to be done where we live and when we live.

With the exception of the names of God and of Christ, no other name is ever associated with the church of God or with churches in the New Testament other than the name of the locality in which they are found. Now, that is a statement that is so true that, of course we all just accept it. But just wait. It is not true today. We find any number of names—Lutheran churches, Anglican churches, Methodist churches, Congregational churches, Mennonite churches, all kinds of things—different names, different personalities. Sometimes the name of some great leader is attached to it. Sometimes the name of a particular teaching is attached to it, like a Holiness church, or a Pentecostal church, or something else. But in the New Testament, you never find anything like this. You never find anything about a Pentecostal church in Colossae, or a Holiness church in Antioch, or a Petrine church in Corinth or an Apollonian church in Jerusalem. It is interesting because when you really begin to look at the Bible, you find only names of the locality are given to the place. For instance, take Revelation 1:11. Jesus is speaking:

... saying, What thou seest, write in a book and send it
to the seven churches: unto Ephesus, and unto Smyrna,
and unto Pergamum, and unto Thyatira, and unto
Sardis, and unto Philadelphia, and unto Laodicea.

Now, if you turn back in your Bible to 1 Thessalonians 1:1 we read this:

Paul, and Silvanus, and Timothy, unto the church of the
Thessalonians in God the Father and the Lord Jesus Christ ...

What a wonderful description: "the church of the Thessalonians in God the Father, and the Lord Jesus Christ." They are there of course, because of the person of the Holy Spirit.

Then again, look at Galatians 1:1–3:

Paul, an apostle (not from men, neither through man, but
through Jesus Christ, and God the Father, who raised him
from the dead) and all the brethren that are with me, unto
the churches of Galatia: Grace to you and peace ...

Or again, look at Philippians 1:1. Now, here we have a slight change, but it is a very interesting change.

Paul and Timothy, servants of Christ Jesus, to all
the saints in Christ Jesus that are at Philippi ...

It is another way of saying the church at Philippi. "... all the saints that are at Philippi ..." Someone will ask, "Oh, how can you say that?" Listen,

... with the bishops and deacons ...

In other words, it is a term synonymous with church. The church at Philippi, with the bishops—that is the elders, and deacons, the overseers, the presbyters. Now again, take another scripture if you want. 1 Corinthians 1:1–2:

Paul, called to be an apostle of Jesus Christ through the will of God, and Sosthenes our brother, unto the church of God which is at Corinth, even them that are sanctified in Christ Jesus, called to be saints, with all that call upon the name of our Lord Jesus Christ in every place, their Lord and ours ...

That is a marvellous little formula, is it not? The church of God which is at Corinth, even those who are sanctified in Christ Jesus, called to be saints with all that call upon the name of the Lord Jesus Christ in every place, every locality, their Lord and ours.

Do you want some more scriptures? Because someone will immediately say, "But just wait, you're talking about the New Testament; those churches weren't so large." Just wait, some of those churches were extremely large, even by modern standards. Look at Acts 8:1, middle part of the verse:

... And there arose on that day a great persecution against the church which was in Jerusalem.

Now the church at Jerusalem numbered 3,000 born again believers on the day of Pentecost (see Acts 2:41). Within a week, it had come to number 5,000 (see Acts 4:4). Within a few more weeks it had numbered a few more thousand. Now, of course, we must understand that some went back home, but even if it was only a church consisting of three or four thousand believers, there was no meeting place in Jerusalem large enough to contain them all! That is why they met in Solomon's porches, in the temple precincts, for prayer and worship and broke bread in homes. A marvellous little comment is made in one place about Peter, that when he was freed, he went to his own company. I find that very interesting. Here are the apostle, he has got his own company. Not meaning his own church, but his own house group. When he was freed from prison, he went immediately to his own, and found them praying. It is so interesting when you begin to see it. You see these are things we overlook. You may not quite see the point at present, but I trust in a moment, you will.

In Acts 2:46, there is the verse that says they met in the temple every day for prayer, and for praise; it also says they broke bread from home to home. And Acts 4:23 is where they went to their own company when they were freed.

Then we have one other very interesting little scripture, which I have often pondered over. Titus 1:5:

For this cause left I thee in Crete, that thou
shouldest set in order the things that are wanting,
and ordain elders in every city ... [KJV]

Now is that not interesting? Not in every church, but in every city. So, it is perfectly clear from the New Testament, that really the only name that was ever associated with a church was the name of its locality. Furthermore, in God's eyes, the church consisted of every born again believer living or resident within that locality. In other words, there was only one church: it was only divided by where you lived. When the apostle Paul was in Antioch, he was in the church at Antioch; when he was in Jerusalem, he was in the church in Jerusalem. He was not a member of the church at Antioch, or in Jerusalem as a visitor. It was only one family. Do you understand? When you begin to see it like that it changes your thinking. You see, the practice of years has so befuddled our thinking on this whole matter of the church, that somehow or other we can only see it through our own experience in these last centuries. But when we get back to the simple, original truth, we make some amazing discoveries.

What is the truth of this matter? It is that there is only one church, only one body of the Lord Jesus, uniting all born again believers into one, whether in heaven or on earth, or wherever we live at the same time, and this oneness must be expressed in time and in place. Indeed, all the work connected with the eternal church, with our being part of the bride of Christ, with our being prepared as the city of God for all eternity has to be done in time on earth, through the church on earth.

Expressing the Church on Earth

How then, do we express this one church? Think for a moment. If we express it racially, we shall have a racially divided church.

We shall have a colour bar—a black church, a white church, a yellow church. No, the Bible says, "no." Shall we divide by nationality? Then we shall have an English church, a Norwegian church, a Swedish church, a German church, a Japanese church, and so on. No, we will not do that. Shall we divide it by social barriers? Then we shall have an upper class church in town and a lower class church in town. We will have those who go to the Salvation Army, and those who will go along to the parish church—those who like something a little more rumbustious and a bit more "music hall-ish" in a way, and those who like something with rather more classical music. We divide it by class. No, we cannot do that. Well, then, shall we divide it by theological emphasis, or Christian personalities? If we do we get denominational churches. That is exactly what they did in Corinth, not the leaders, but the people. They were divided. Some said, "I am of Apollos." Others said, "I am of Cephas," and others said, "I am of Paul." There was a group who called themselves "the exclusives." They said, "We are of Christ, and we exclude all the others. We don't have anything to do with them; they're just fleshly." But the apostle Paul said, "Is Christ divided?" He cannot be divided, there is only one Christ. It does not matter if you say you are of Paul, you are still in the one Christ, who is bigger than those who say, "I am of Paul" and those who say, "I am of Apollos." He is bigger than that group." He includes those of Paul, and includes those of Peter, as well as the exclusives.

If you think for a moment, there is only one way in which you can divide the church and not do it along naturally divisive lines, and that is locality. As soon as you divide the church by where we live in the area—the municipality, the locality, whatever you like to call it, the city, the town in which we live— immediately, we are all one. It is not a question of being Chinese, Japanese, English, Swedish, Finnish, or Russian. It is a question of you being in Christ. If you are here in Richmond, you are in the church here in Richmond. If you are in Moscow, you will be in the church in Moscow. If you are in Tokyo, you will be in the church in Tokyo.

Now, of course, there must be problems here because we have huge urban areas, such as New York, such as Los Angeles, such as London, such as Tokyo, such as Shanghai. What should we do? Long ago, this matter was faced by some brethren and they said, I think quite rightly, the best thing to do is to take the municipal areas within the city and make them separate entities. There is really no other way. However, without being legalistic, this matter is very important because the only foundation for the practical gathering together and building up of the church is Christ. It is not a geographical locality. It is Christ. But then we must say, it is Christ as He is found in the locality in which I live. Otherwise, I run right across London to a company I like. That is not good enough. It means I am not facing up to the issues in my life. "There is someone in that company I cannot bear! So, I would much prefer to run off to Richmond, where I am not really known, where I can sit in peace. But you are not facing up to the reality. It is all very well for us to have draped across our platform "All one in Christ Jesus," when we are not at all one. We are at each other's throats, scratching out each other's eyes. We cannot sit together, we cannot worship together, we cannot take communion together. So, we have to run off elsewhere. That is not good enough. God traps us into the area where we live and then we have to face up to all the problems that are within us.

You see, dear child of God, you may get very upset about this, but in the end, you will have to face it. The real problem is not others, it is you. The real problem is not others, it is me. I can often say, "If I didn't have those others, I'd be a marvellous saint." But God says, "Oh no. If you were a marvellous saint, you would feel it in your attitude to those difficult people." They are the means by which saints are made. Run away from it, and you lose all possibility of being conformed to the image of God's Son. You run into that awful realm, which is so common in evangelical circles, where we learn and learn and learn and learn and learn and never arrive. So, this is no small matter. Are you in Christ? Then you must find your brothers and sisters in Christ where you live and be built up with them. Upon that foundation alone, the Spirit of God begins to build living stone together with living stone. It is not the ones we like, but the ones ordained by God for us. He knits member to member.

It is very simple really, the way He does it. The Spirit there puts everything to the acid test, training us, disciplining us, educating us, qualifying us. For instance, you say that you have love in your heart for the Lord, then you must say at times, well, I love God's people. But the acid test is whether you can really work together with others in a team, and with people who rub you the wrong way. Then, you will know whether the love of God is really in your heart or whether it is sentimentality. You will know whether you want a social club where people like you and you like them, or whether you really mean business with God and really want to be conformed to the image of God's Son.

We can talk about supporting evangelisation schemes, we can say, "I pray for missionaries on the other side of the world," but when it comes to going out on a Sunday evening into the streets, we are never found there. When it comes even to our presence in a time that is directed towards others, we are never there. We can talk until we are blue in the face about our great missionary burden, but unless in the acid test of the local, it is seen to be a genuine burden for other human beings, it is hogwash. If a person cannot even give themselves in prayer for evangelistic endeavour, what is the point of our saying that they support missionaries somewhere else in some other part of the world? In the end, this all comes down, in the final analysis, to the way we come through where we live.

Now, this matter of living within the locality is thus of vital importance. Do not compromise over it. Do not allow the pressure of circumstances to influence you into compromising. I have seen it again and again. You young married ones, you will find it a thousand times easier to get a place just outside the area rather than within it. The devil will make sure about that. Then most people will come and say, "Well, what can we do? Don't we need a home?" Of course. But you see, no one ever thinks of the problems. In some places, every member of the family has a car, but what happens if that is not the case? What happens when you have a family? How do you really get in for fellowship? Wives are cut off. It is very well to talk about this and some will say, "You know, we can get there very easily; we can do this. We are on a bus route." Then what happens when we have an energy crisis? Nothing runs.

We are moving into the period of what the Bible calls, in Matthew 24, famines. Most people have always thought of these famines as being shortages of food. They have never realised that it is just famines. Shortages. Shortages of petrol, shortages of other raw goods, all kinds of things. We are moving into that era, so this matter of where we live is very important. Do not compromise over it, or you may find that because you compromised on something which you knew to be true, you are caught when the crisis comes. Then the excuses you made will mock you. The devil will see to that. God never communicates truth to be compromised. He communicates truth to be obeyed in faith. I have never known anyone who has responded to light given to them in faith, with the obedience of faith, who has lived to regret it. Every time I hear, again and again, people say later, "Thank God, I did that. At the time I had such a battle, but thank God, now I understand it. Isn't it amazing? I did this and this and now see what has happened."

I trust that what I say really does find a home in your heart. In times of national or international crisis or strife—the emergencies which we are beginning to experience as well as war—it is a very important thing that we be found within the kind of area where the saints live so that we can contact one another, if necessary, by walking around. Supposing in the end, the third World War does come. What about folks that are far away? They have never been able to get to know the saints there. Then, what do we do? We cannot walk to them, we cannot cycle 'round to them. But if they are within the area, somewhere, there will be people who are near enough just to pop by and see that so and so is alright. This whole matter is not so stupid as it may seem. It is not something to be played about with. We have been given some years of grace. In these years of grace, we need to wake up and not be foolish virgins, who suddenly when the moment comes say, "Oh!" and rush off, "Please help us now to do something."

We will not be able to do anything when the crisis comes. Everyone will be busy looking after their own families.

So do not take this matter lightly. The mystery of Christ has to be experienced and expressed locally. It is there that the real work is done whereby we practically experience what it is to be fellow-heirs, fellow-members of the body, fellow-partakers. There, we discover the reality of it and, by the grace of God, we overcome.

The Vehicle to Express Christ's Headship

Now I would like to go on to another matter, which is also just as important, in fact, in many ways, I would say it is even more important. It is this: the vehicle for the Headship of Christ to be known and expressed. Or, if you like, use the word experienced and expressed. The mystery of Christ is that we have been made fellow-members of the body of which He is the head. In practical terms, therefore, it is the Headship of Christ in powerful, actual, and concrete action. Did you understand that? In practical terms, this union with Christ functions, grows, and is fulfilled. The purpose of God is realised through it, through the Headship of Jesus Christ. His authority, is not a theory or an ideal, but is to be experienced in practical terms.

The body of Christ, the church, has only one head. Now, I think we all know that Colossians 1:18 says that He (that is Jesus) is the head of the body, which is the church, that in all things He might have the preeminence. In Ephesians 1:22, it says, "subjecting all things under His feet, and gave Him, that is Jesus, to be head over everything to the church, which is His body, the fullness of Him who fills all in all." Only one head, through the person of the Holy

Spirit, the authority of Christ, His mind, His will, His thoughts, are to be practically communicated to the church—practically communicated. You see, this is the whole crux of the matter.

Every single movement of the Holy Spirit, right from the day of Pentecost, right the way through the long story of the church, has been that when the Holy Spirit has moved, there have been men and women who have acknowledged the Headship and Lordship of Jesus Christ alone. On that day of Pentecost, suddenly, 120 units of a congregation became 120 members of a body. When Peter stood up to speak, the 11 stood up automatically with him, and he was their mouthpiece. There was no more rivalry. They were not saying, "Who is the greatest? Who has the anointing?" John did not say, "Why shouldn't I, John, speak?" or James say, "Why shouldn't I, James, speak? Why should he [Peter] speak?! Wasn't he the one who denied the Lord three times with oaths and curses?" No, they became a body. It did not bother them anymore. As long as it was the Lord speaking, they did not mind that their mouth had been shut. If he spoke, they were speaking. He was their mouth! They were members of a body. For the first time they felt: we are in this together. We do not mind who God uses, so long as He does the work.

It is so at every other time in church history. In the Reformation, in the Puritan period, later on in the Quakers, and later on in the Methodists, then in the great Brethren movement, and then the Pentecostal movement. All the way through church history it has been the same, that whenever the Spirit of God has moved, one of the evidences of it have been men and women who have owned, absolutely, without reservation or condition, the Lordship of Jesus. The Holy Spirit has communicated the mind of the risen head to

His body, and then something has happened. Every single time, the Headship of Jesus Christ has been substituted by man or men, whether a council of men, or one man or two or three men, then immediately, the whole thing has crystallised and died. You can dress it up in biblical terms and make it sound very, very correct, but if a man, even if it is a Bible pattern, puts his head in the place of the Lord Jesus, the church is effectively paralysed. There is no more growth, no more function, and no more movement. But as soon as that substitute is out of the way, and the Lord Jesus can speak, and His people hear and obey, immediately it is renewal.

That the Lord Jesus could direct the church on earth, is often considered mystical and impractical. In fact, people consider it impossible. They say that, "Don't be silly, God's given us common sense. How could the Lord Jesus direct the church on earth?" Well, then what does the Bible mean? What does it mean when it says again and again and again and again that He is head of the church? Is it just an ideal? Is He just a figurehead, like the Queen? A constitutional monarch? We write their speeches for them. We pass the laws, but they have to sign them. They are just a figurehead. It is us who are doing it all really. We are speaking, we are acting, we are working, we are enacting the laws and regulations, but we use their name, the stamp of their authority. Is that what the church is? Or in the Book, when it says that Jesus is head, does it really mean that He is practically head, that there is the mind of God in Him, there is the will of God in Him, there are the thoughts of God in Him, there is the Word of God in Him and therefore it has to be communicated to us for obedience.

I do not understand this talk of the Headship of Christ being mystical, impossible, impractical. It goes to the very root of the gospel. If it is mystical, impractical, or impossible, then let us give up. What was the church on the day of Pentecost? It turned Jerusalem upside down. Why? Because the risen head was directing it through the Holy Spirit. He directed it through Judea, then Samaria, then through to the uttermost parts of the earth. Even Rome crumbles into the dust and that despised movement of the Spirit of God spreads throughout the whole Roman Empire until, in the end, the Roman Empire is a shadow of history ... but the church is with us today.

Now, my point is this. It does not matter whether it is a man or a collection of men who substitute the Headship of Christ for their own. Whoever does it, in the end, destroys the growth, the function, and the fulfilment of the church. I do not want to upset anybody, but let me just go over the whole gamut. It can be popes, or cardinals, or archbishops, or bishops. It can be synods. It can be moderators or pastors or vicars. It can be elders, or deacons. It can be dictatorship or autocracy—one man holding everything in his hands and commanding the whole hierarchy. Or it can be democracy and congregational business meetings, based virtually on a common opinion of the majority without any regard to what the mind of God might be in a given situation. It can be something totally unbiblical, something un-New Testament or it can be a New Testament pattern, so polished and so perfect that it is impossible to fault. But whatever it is, if it puts its head in the place of the Lord Jesus Christ, it is sinful. Oh, that is terribly strong, right? Yes—I say it is sinful, because anything which paralyses the building work of the Lord Jesus is sinful. Thank God, if a pope gets on his knees and gets his direction from God, you know something could happen in the

Catholic church—and something is happening, to the shock of many evangelicals. I have in myself no doubt that our present pope [Pope John Paul II] is a real believer, born of God. When the group, the Living Sound¹ came to Krakow in Poland, he personally introduced them, giving his testimony when he was archbishop of Krakow.

You can get a sound Baptist pastor who puts his head in the place of the Lord, or a bunch of born again deacons who put their heads in the place of the Lord Jesus and effectively destroy the church's growth and function. You also could conceivably have a pope, or a cardinal, or an archbishop who so bowed before the Lord that the Lord could find a way right through them to renew and quicken and start something moving that would have untold consequences.

It is the church's responsibility to be subject to its head. In Ephesians 5, it puts it very simply, I think most of you will know it very well. But maybe you have never actually noticed it in this connection in Ephesians 5:24:

But as the church is subject to Christ, so let
the wives also be to their husbands ...

Well, for one moment, forget the last part about wives being subject to their husbands, although of course, it is absolutely right, but just get this first part clear. Listen to this:

... as the church is subject to Christ.

---

1 An American gospel group dedicated to witnessing about their new life in Jesus Christ [1975].

It is the responsibility of the church to be subject to its Lord, to its head. The Holy Spirit has come in order to make that a powerful and practical reality. I think the person of the Holy Spirit is so wonderful in this matter. He waits and He waits and He waits for the opportunity to make a powerful dynamic reality of the Headship of Jesus. There are so few places where the Holy Spirit is able to do this. But when the opportunity is given to the Holy Spirit, if I may be so irreverent as to say, He almost falls over Himself to communicate the mind of the Lord Jesus.

I want you just to consider a few scriptures, if you will take the Book and look at these. I think most of you will know them, but have you ever thought of them in this connection? Listen to this in Ephesians 4:15–16. This is all about the body of Jesus:

> but speaking truth in love, may grow up in all
> things into him, who is the head, even Christ; from
> whom all the body fitly framed and knit together
> through that which every joint supplieth ...

Now, I want you just to underline this: "growing up into Him, as head, even Christ from whom all the body ..." How can we know the body functioning? How can we know the maintenance of the oneness of the body? How can we possibly know the realisation of the purpose of God through the body, unless we grow up into Him as head? What does it mean, growing up into Him as head? I think that is a most fascinating phrase. It does not say, *recognise* Him as head. That is true. That is initial. It does not say, *confess* Him as head, as Lord. That is absolutely foundational. It says, "grow up into Him as head." It seems to suggest that we, as members of the Lord Jesus together in Christ, in a locality, should *grow* up together into Him as head. Finding out what it is to know the mind of the Lord together, how to read the mind of the Lord, how to sense the mind of the Lord, and how to obey the mind of the Lord. When we begin to grow up into Him as head, when we get our relationship with Him clear, then we can get our relationship with one another clear. As I grow up into Him as head, I find the body. "... from whom all the body ..."

So often in these movements that I call church type movements or New Testament pattern movements, they have got hold of a New Testament pattern and they want to try and put it into operation. You will find again and again, they go at it on the horizontal. "Okay, let's find the body. Let's get the members. Let's get everybody together. Let's set up the church. We'll have the Lord's table and we'll have elders and deacons. We'll sort out a few elders, and we'll sort out a few for deacons." This kind of way of doing is all on the horizontal. God does not do it that way. He does it in the vertical. We only know the body growing, functioning, and every part supplying something, as we grow up into Him as head. There is a process. There is a progressive experience. There is some way in which we have got to find one another in Him.

Now, let us go on to another scripture in this matter. In Colossians 2:19, there is another very well-known phrase, this time it is put in the negative way:

and not holding fast the Head, from whom all the
body, being supplied and knit together through the joints
and bands, increaseth with the increase of God.

Now this is interesting: "holding fast the Head, from whom all the body ..." so the first thing is "growing up into the head, even Christ." Here is another, "holding fast the head from whom the body." If you try to hold fast to your brothers and sisters, you will lose them. What will happen will be this: if you do not lose them, they will all be lost together. I could never believe that movement of God, the Brethren movement, which was really in its beginning so remarkable, and then the exclusive movement which had such depth, even though I do not personally agree with exclusive-ism at all, should have ended up the way it has. Could you believe that a whole group could move together, holding together ... away and away and away from the head? As they held to one another, and all watched one another: "Is it the party line? Are we doing the right thing?" So, they all moved away. The children of God have done the same thing. What began as a real work of God has veered away and away and away. Until now we hear their leaders talking about Gaddafi as a prophet of God. It is incredible, is it not and we say, "Well, how could this happen? These are groups that saw something." Yes, but they went on the horizontal, not the vertical. They did not "grow up into Him, who is the head, even Christ, from whom all the body ..." They did not "hold fast the head from whom the whole body ..." They tried to find the body first and then tried to hold the body, tried to set up something and so went off the rails.

How is His Headship Experienced?

Now, what does this mean? How do you grow up into Him who is the head, even Christ? How do you hold fast the head and find the body? How do we experience this? May I just say it very simply:

our problem is so often centred on how far we should identify divine authority with human authority. Do you understand what I am trying to get at? We can all say, "Oh, yes, yes, I accept the Lordship of Jesus Christ. But sometimes when the elders say something, I have a problem. Now, I say! I didn't like that ... well ... I don't accept that. That wasn't the Lord." So, what do we do? Isn't our problem in how far we identify divine authority with the human vessel?

Now, I think there are some tragedies in the country and in the world at large on this matter. We have whole hierarchical systems that have been built. We have this pyramid kind of system. We have this insistence on people covenanting, obeying, submitting. But we must be very careful that we do not go to the other extreme and, as we say, throw out the baby with the bathwater. There is some truth there.

For instance, let me give you a problem. Take Hebrews 13:17:

Obey them that have the rule over you ...

Well, you cannot get away from that, can you? Now would you please notice this phrase first, "have the rule over you." Now, it is a rather authoritarian type of phrase is it not? "Have the rule ..." There are people who have the rule over you. "Oh, dear. I wish you hadn't said that. Everything was lovely in this Bible study up to now. I mean, we don't mind sort of recognising Jesus as Lord, as head. But I want to decide what the head is saying. I want to determine." What does it mean "have the rule over you? Oh, you say, "Well, maybe it's only one place. Never build a doctrine on one place." Just wait. Verse seven:

Remember them that had the rule over you, men that
spake unto you the word of God; and considering
the issue of their life, imitate their faith.

Oh, just wait just in case you think you can get away with it?
Verse 24:

Salute all them that have the rule over you

Oh dear. It is like the needle has got stuck. "... have the rule
over you ..." three times in one portion? I mean, it cannot be a
mistake, can it? Somehow or other, the Holy Spirit is trying to say
something: there are people who have the rule over you.

Then, notice the second thing: "obey." That is a very authoritarian
type of word. You think: "I do not like that word. *Understand*—that
is a nicer word, or *cogitate* on those who have the rule over you.
I don't like that word obey." But think about it.

Here is the third thing, just in case we get a kind of slavish
idea of this authority. It says, "considering the issue of their life,
imitate their faith." Remember. Consider. Imitate. In other words,
those who have the rule over you should at least have a little
more of the Lord. Something to remember, something to consider,
something to imitate. It is not just dictatorship. There is some
spiritual seniority.

Now, there are some other scriptures if you want to just take
note of them. I Thessalonians 5:12:

But we beseech you, brethren, to know them that
labor among you, and are over you in the Lord ...

Oh, that is kindly put. This is the apostle Paul. (I am not at all myself convinced that the writer of the Hebrew letter was the apostle Paul). But here is the apostle Paul, always more gentle in his ways. He does not say *have the rule over you*, but, he says, "... them that are over you in the Lord ..." just a little more gentle. But it still is them that are over you. Now, notice again what it says:

> But we beseech you, brethren, to know them that labor among
> you, and are over you in the Lord, and admonish you;

"Admonish you." Oh, we do not always like that either, do we? Oh, you know, sometimes we get very upset that the brothers never say anything to us! But if they were always admonishing us, I do not think we would like that. Admonishing—something else to think about, is it not?

Now, what about 1 Corinthians 16:15–16?

> Now I beseech you, brethren (ye know the house of
> Stephanas, that it is the firstfruits of Achaia, and
> that they have set themselves to minister unto the
> saints), that ye also be in subjection unto such, and to
> every one that helpeth in the work and laboreth.

"Oh, you mean, not only the elders, but '... every one that helpeth in the work and laboreth?' Oh dear. I can see trouble; problems. It is a discipline here. I do not like that word in subjection. That is not a nice word. In subjection!"

Mind you, it does say that these people minister unto the saints, which is beautiful. In other places it says, "They washed their feet." Lovely. But we have to be in subjection to such. "Oh dear, do you mean everybody who has got responsibility in the work that we should ... we should ...?" Yes.

"Oh, dear. Now I can understand what you mean about this problem of divine authority in the human vessel. I don't mind being under the government of the Lord, so long as I can determine what the government of the Lord is. But if someone is going to tell me, 'Would you do this' or 'you didn't do that right,' I don't like that."

Now, look at another scripture. 1 Peter 5:1–5:

> *The elders therefore among you I exhort, who am a fellow-*
> *elder, and a witness of the sufferings of Christ, who am*
> *also a partaker of the glory that shall be revealed: Tend the*
> *flock of God which is among you, exercising the oversight,*

I like that word oversight. It somehow speaks of the whole flock functioning does it not? There are those who have oversight; they have an overall view, watching the whole. It is not that they do all the work. It is rather that they watch over the functioning of the whole. Then it goes on:

> *not of constraint, but willingly, according to the will*
> *of God; nor yet for filthy lucre [that is, because they*
> *get a nice pay packet], but of a ready mind; neither*
> *as lording it over [the flock] the charge allotted to*
> *you, but making yourselves ensamples to the flock.*

The Word of God is wonderful because it keeps us from all these excesses we see in church history and on the contemporary scene. I see men sometimes lording it over the flock. You know, building whole empires, everyone there has got to do exactly what they are talking about, not knowing whether it is really right. However, there is a place for those who have the rule over us.

I have only talked about elders, deacons, and those in the work; now I want to come to something else. What about apostolic authority? Well, there is such a thing as apostolic authority. Listen to what the apostle says, in II Corinthians 10:8:

For though I should glory somewhat abundantly
concerning our authority (which the Lord gave for
building you up, and not for casting you down) ...

What is the apostle Paul talking about? "Authority given to us, not to cast you down, but to build you up?" He says it again in 13:10:

For this cause I write these things while absent, that I may not
when present deal sharply, according to the authority which
the Lord gave me for building up, and not for casting down.

So, there is apostolic authority. Oh, dear, that means that there is such a thing as apostolic authority. It means that a man with much wider responsibility and authority than a local church can, in fact, say something to a local church. Now, the interesting thing is this, that those churches had the freedom to turn away, and they did. So, we have to get this quite clear. It was no hierarchical system where an apostle can turn them all out of the building or whatever. You see, you cannot exercise authority unless people give you authority. It is very true. You cannot exercise authority unless people give you authority. The rest becomes a slavish dictatorship out of which all life and love depart.

Now, I want you to note, one wonderful little thing that has always been a great deliverance to me. It is a very well-known verse, but people never tend to realise what it is saying. Ephesians 2:20:

being built upon the foundation of the apostles and
prophets, Christ Jesus himself being the chief corner stone;

Now here is something I find just wonderful! Because there is a kind of idea of authority that has always got the pyramid with the big men, the top brass, right on the top, sitting there. Then down you come from apostles to prophets, and then you come to elders, deacons, and then all the poor flock squashed underneath. They have to obey what comes from above. I do not find it in the Book. I find the whole thing inverted. I find that the apostles and prophets are a foundation upon which the whole solid weight of the building rests. What pressure! What burdens! Ahh, that is a different thing.

Years ago, when Norman Grubb came back from the Far East, that was the first time I ever had a long talk with him. I remember him saying how enthralled he was with what he found in the Far East and in India. I listened, enraptured. We had been so ostracised for so many years, that the very fact that he wanted to talk with us, I thought was so lovely. Of course, I came to the Lord through the book he wrote, so naturally I felt I doubly owed something to him. But I was so thrilled to hear him talking, in rapturous terms about what he had seen. "It was," he said, "the church in action." But then he suddenly stopped and coughed and said, "But, I am not sure that there is not a fatal weakness."

So, I looked at him aghast! I said, "Fatal weakness? What do you mean?"

He said, "The view of authority."

"Oh, no!" I said.

"Oh, well," he said, "I may be wrong, I may be wrong."

"Oh, actually," I said, "I think you are." I said, "I mean, we live in these days of anarchy and loss."

"Well," he said, "as I see it, I think there is such a delicate balance between the people of God and those who have this kind of apostolic authority."

He was right. It was the fatal flaw and what has happened to that movement is because there was a fatal flaw in the concept of authority. We are seeing the same thing now because people never learn. You know, Mark Twain said, "We learn from history that we never learn from history." We are doomed to make the same historic mistakes again and again because we never learn. It is a shame. To me, this whole matter of authority is, as our Lord Jesus put it so beautifully, in Mark 10:42–45:

> *And Jesus called them to him, and saith unto them, Ye know that they who are accounted to rule over the Gentiles lord it over them; and their great ones exercise authority over them. But it is not so among you: but whosoever would become*

great among you, shall be your minister; [bondslave, that is a hired servant] *and whosoever would be first among you, shall be* [bondslave] *of all.* [That is, no time off.] *For the Son of man also came not to be ministered unto, but to minister, and to give his life a ransom for many.*

You see, that we might reign with Christ in the ages to come and be part of His eternal government and come to sit with Him in the throne and share in His administration, a very large and necessary part of our training, of that discipline, of that education is involved with our relationship to those who have the rule over us, who have responsibility for us. On the other hand, lest we get a wrong idea, an unbalanced picture, a top-heavy view of authority, we should consider the scriptures, which I feel are a tremendous corrective to a wrong idea of authority. Ephesians 5:21:

... subjecting yourselves one to another in the fear of Christ.

I think it is beautiful. It says, "Be filled with the Spirit," and then it says, "subject yourselves one to another." What does it mean subject yourselves? If we are members of a body, how can we act as if there is no body? "Oh," you say, "I wouldn't act as if there's no body!" Oh yes, you would. I would do the same. It is the natural thing.

Suppose my little finger said, "I'm off to Timbuktu."

"You're off to Timbuktu? How can you? You're in the body? Don't you feel any relationship to the rest? Maybe you should go to Timbuktu, but don't you think that at least you should share it?"

You know, it's amazing. I have never failed to be amazed when people suddenly come and announce, "We're moving to the Isle of Wight next week."

"Oh really?"

"Yes, the Lord's arranged it all." Oh, that is strange, is it not? Living stones are supposed to be built together and suddenly one living stone goes ... out! Off! Members knit together, functioning, growing up into Christ who is the head and suddenly we discover they are gone! It is very odd. It is not that the church wants to dictate, but surely there should be some sense inside, subjecting yourselves to one another. In the end, is it not for your security? If the church is wise, it will never direct you. But you know, we change homes, we change jobs, we do all kinds of things. You may think, "Why? The church has got far more important matters to pray about." Yes. But do you not think that the enemy will say, "Out. You, there. You, there." Before long, there is no more building.

"Submitting yourselves one to another in the fear of Christ." I like that word, the fear of Christ, in the reverence of Christ, in the fear of the Lordship of Christ. In other words, do not be so big-headed to think that you have necessarily got, dogmatically, the mind of God for you. For your security, open up to the family. It is all part of "growing up into Him who is the head from whom all the body is fitly framed." We belong to one another. We cannot just say farewell to one another like that. There is some kind of relationship isn't there? You see, you will find it in all kinds of things if you want to look at it. There is Philippians 2:3, which says it this way:

*... doing nothing through faction or through vainglory, but in
lowliness of mind each counting others better than himself ...*

Your older versions say "esteeming others better than yourself."
The feeling is, do not despise your brothers and sisters. Esteem
them as having at least something of the Lord more than you,
and go on the basis that they love you.

Shall I tell you something? I found in the past I was so afraid
to ask about something because I felt, "Oh, so-and-so is bound
to manipulate and so-and-so has cast-iron views, they won't
agree with that." Then when finally you get through and you
open up, you find to your amazement that people treat you very,
very sensitively. It seems that if you trust your brothers and
sisters, they trust you. When you distrust them, they distrust you.
I often think it is the same with the Lord. It says, "with the froward,
He is froward." Remember? So, I think this is a very important
thing.

Look at another scripture Galatians 5:13:

*For ye, brethren, were called for freedom; only use
not your freedom for an occasion to the flesh, but
through love be servants one to another.*

Is it not the same thought all over again? Then 1 Peter 5:5:

*Likewise, ye younger, be subject unto the elder. [Now,
listen to this]: Yea, all of you gird yourselves with
humility, to serve one another: for God resisteth
the proud, but giveth grace to the humble.*

Now, we could say a lot more about all this matter. There are times where an apostle should submit to the church. There are times when elders should submit to the church. It is all part of growing up into Him who is the head. You see, God does not always automatically reveal His mind to those who are apostles, or those who are elders. Sometimes it comes through the simplest, humblest members of the body. When we are all seeking to know what is the way, suddenly it begins to filter out and the elders define it. It is not that they are always *telling* the church what is the mind of God, they should, in fact, be *expressing* what is in the heart of the church because the whole mind of God is in us all. We all know the Lord from the least to the greatest. Now, if we are members of Christ and members one of another, well then, should we not submit ourselves one to another? Can one member act as if there are no other members?

So, in a world of growing lawlessness and anarchy, greater and greater rebellion, against all rule and authority, the church on earth is to be the sphere and the realm where the rule and authority of God is experienced and expressed. When the world touches us, it should not touch faction, disorder, unrest, rebellion, but it should touch life, order, and fulfilment. That is the whole thing about having good central authority, is it not? Do you not think that? When there was no king in the land, everybody did that which was right in their own eyes. What a terrible thing it is, when central authority begins to break down, and the whole country begins to break up. It is terrible. Why do we have authority? That we may be able to live, that we might be fulfilled. That is why the church needs to be a microcosm of the kingdom of God on earth, a little colony of heaven, in which the reign and rule of God is experienced and expressed.

I do trust that somehow you all begin to understand. That is why, when the Lord spoke about building the church, He spoke about giving us the keys of the kingdom. That is why it says in Psalm 110 that He will rule in the midst of His enemies. He will lift up the rod of His strength out of Zion. That is why we are called priests and kings. We are meant to rule here. It is not only that we are to know in our midst the rule of God, but that through us, the Lord Jesus could rule over nations, over our nation, and over the area in which we are found. It is not only just that we might know the rule of God amongst ourselves, it is that we become a vehicle by which the Lord Jesus can rule over a nation. We have to be the light of the world, exposing darkness, bringing in the mind of God for those who have a heart for Him. We are supposed to be a city set up on a hill. What is a city? It is a place of administration, set on a hill so that the world can see that is what it should be like. We are meant to be the salt of the earth, stopping corruption. This is what we are meant to be. We cannot be that unless the Headship of Jesus Christ is known by every member.

May the Lord help us then in this vital matter. We have talked about two very practical and vital matters. Do you want to come to the throne? Do you want to be part of that city? Do you want to reign with Christ in the ages to come? Then, there is a sphere of education here. There is a realm of discipline here. There is this school of training here. It is not easy, but if we look to God, He will give us the grace. We will be eternally thankful to Him. Shall we pray?

Now, Lord, we have really covered some ground here. We have covered very important ground, Lord, and it is very easy for us to just listen, and not really retain. Now, Lord, we commit it all back to Thee. By Thy Spirit, Lord, make this flesh and blood. Apply Thy Word to us, Lord. In this whole matter of really being built together, help us Lord, we pray. Lord, we pray that Thou wilt likewise help us in this whole tremendous and vital matter connected with Thy Headship. Lord, may we all know Thee as Lord, not in word, but in practice and we ask this together, in the name of our Lord Jesus. Amen.

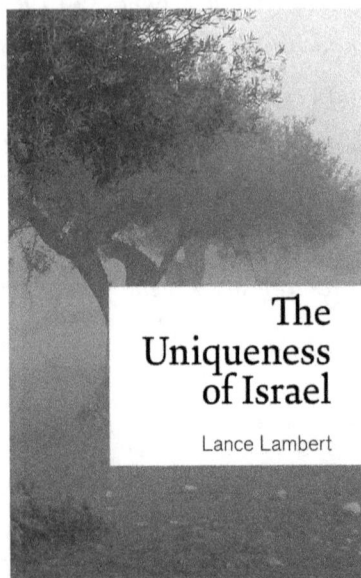

The
Uniqueness
of Israel

Lance Lambert

The Uniqueness of Israel

Woven into the fabric of Jewish existence there is an undeniable uniqueness. There is bitter controversy over the subject of Israel, but time itself will establish the truth about this nation's place in God's plan. For Lance Lambert, the Lord Jesus is the key that unlocks Jewish history He is the key not only to their fall, but also to their restoration. For in spite of the fact that they rejected Him, He has not rejected them.

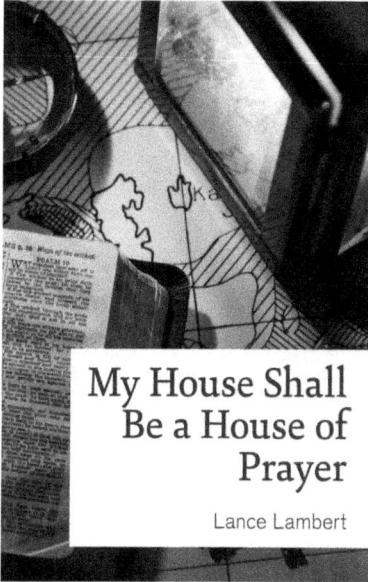

My House Shall
Be a House of
Prayer

Lance Lambert

My House Shall Be a House of Prayer

As the return of the Lord draws near there has never been a time when effective prayer is more strategic, necessary, and essential than now. Will we be a people who will truly watch and pray? Will anyone respond to His call and challenge? Corporate intercession is almost a lost art—and that when we most need it!

> I sought for a man among them, that should build up the wall, and stand in the gap before me for the land, that I should not destroy it; but I found none (Ezekiel 22:30).

This is the call and challenge of the Lord.

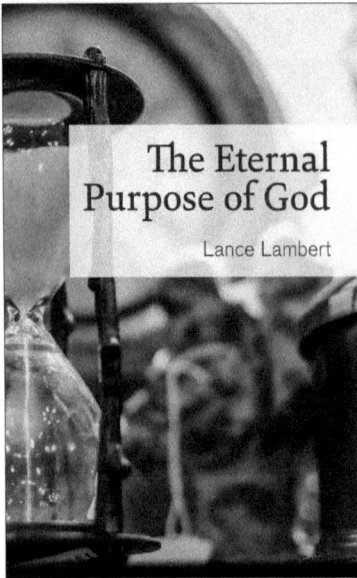

The Eternal Purpose of God

There is no truth that is of greater importance than this matter of God's eternal purpose. Once you begin to understand God's ultimate aim in time, and for the ages to come, life becomes more meaningful and significant. Why did God create this universe and this earth, which at our present extent of knowledge is unique? What was His aim and goal in its creation? Why did He create mankind? And when man fell short of His glory through sin, why did He persevere and provide salvation? Is that salvation an end in itself, or is it a means to an end, with everything provided within it to reach the final goal? And how can I be involved in the fulfillment of that purpose?

This book is a helpful response to these questions, revealing the heart of God.

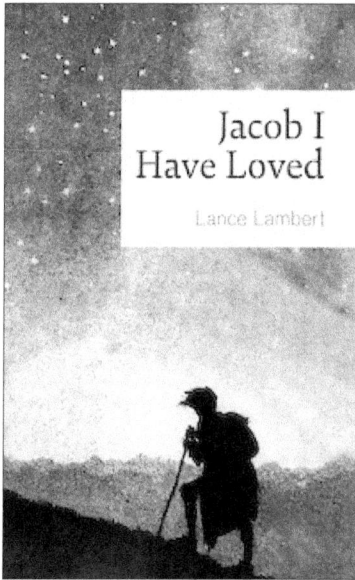

Jacob I Have Loved

When God deals with us it is often in deeply mystifying ways. There is no greater example of how God shapes a person than through the remarkable story of Jacob. It is an outstanding illustration of God's desire to utterly transform our fallen inner nature. Despite a twisted, deceiving, and sinful heart, Jacob nonetheless inherited God's richest blessings and became one of the patriarchs of our faith. Herein lies one of the Bible's great mysteries. The amazing truth is that Jacob's name has not been lost in the debris of human history, nor has it been forgotten, as have so many other names. Incredibly, it is forever linked with God. His story is an integral part of the history of divine redemption. This book is about the power of God to transform a human life.

Jacob's story is our story.

www.ingramcontent.com/pod-product-compliance
Lightning Source LLC
LaVergne TN
LVHW051301080426
835509LV00020B/3093